CONTENTS

IMMUNE BOOSTING SMOOTHIES

Creamy Pink Smoothie

Servings: 2
Cooking Time: 5 Minutes
Ingredients:
- 2 cups strawberries (fresh or frozen)
- 2 tablespoon cashew butter
- 1 ½ cup of almond milk (unsweetened)
- 2 tablespoons rolled oats
- 1 teaspoon vanilla extract
- 1 teaspoon raw organic honey
- A pinch of cinnamon power
- 1 teaspoon of cashew flakes (garnish)

Directions:
1. Place all the ingredients in your blender and run it on high for 1 minute.
2. Pour into serving glasses and top it with a sprinkle of cashew flakes.
3. Enjoy!

Kiwi- Banana Healer

Servings: 1
Cooking Time: 5 Minutes
Ingredients:
- 1 kiwi, peeled and chopped
- ¼ avocado, chopped
- 1 Swiss chard leaf,
- 1 small frozen banana
- 1 cup coconut water
- 1 teaspoon Spirulina powder
- 2 tablespoon hemp seeds
- 3-4 ice cubes

Directions:
1. Add all the ingredients one by one into your blender and process until smooth.
Nutrition Info: (Per Serving): Calories- 365, Fat-14 g, Protein- 11 g, carbohydrates- 47 g

Papaya Passion

Servings: 1
Cooking Time: 2 Minutes
Ingredients:
- 1 cup papaya, chopped
- ½ cup pineapple, peeled and chopped
- 1 cup, low fat or fat free yogurt (plain)
- 1 teaspoon coconut oil
- 1 teaspoon flaxseed powder
- A handful of ice

Directions:
1. Add the papaya, pineapple and ice into your blender and process it on medium high speed till well combined.
2. Next add the coconut oil, flaxseed powder and yogurt and process it on high speed for 1 minutes till you get a creamy, thick mixture.
3. Serve chilled!
Nutrition Info: (Per Serving): Calories-300, Fat-1.5 g, Protein- 13 g, Carbohydrates- 65 g

Orange Coco Smoothie

Servings: 2
Cooking Time: 10 Minutes
Ingredients:
*   1 cup freshly squeezed orange juice
*   6 California tangerines, peeled and chopped
*   1 cup mixed greens
*   2 teaspoons freshly grated ginger root
*   Juice of 2 freshly squeezed lemons
*   1 ½ cups of coconut milk/ coconut water (your choice)
*   4 teaspoons pure coconut oil
*   2 tablespoons Chia seeds
*   4 teaspoons raw organic honey
*   1 tablespoons any super food of your choice

Directions:
1. To your blender jar, add all the ingredients in the given order and whirr it up for 90 seconds or until done.
Nutrition Info: (Per Serving): Calories-267, Fat-1.3 g, Protein-5.3 g, Carbohydrates- 68.4 g

Multi-berry Smoothie

Servings: 1
Cooking Time: 5 Minutes
Ingredients:
*   1 cup almond/ cashew milk
*   2 blood oranges, peeled and chopped
*   ½ teaspoon vanilla extract
*   ½ cup mixed berries (fresh or frozen)
*   ½ avocado, peeled and chopped
*   ½ tablespoon cacao powder
*   ½ tablespoon coconut oil

Directions:
1. Pour all the ingredients into your blender and whizz it up till the desired consistency is reached.
Nutrition Info: (Per Serving): Calories- 265, Fat-10 g, Protein- 10 g, Carbohydrates-30 g

Cacao- Spirulina And Berry Booster

Servings: 1
Cooking Time: 5 Minutes
Ingredients:
- 1 banana, (fresh or frozen)
- 1 cup coconut milk
- 1 cup strawberries (fresh or frozen)
- 1 cup mixed greens
- ½ cup blueberries (frozen)
- 1 teaspoon cacao powder
- 1 teaspoon Spirulina powder
- ½ tablespoon coconut oil
- A large pinch of cinnamon powder
- 1 teaspoon of raw, organic honey,
- 1 tablespoon of any super food of your choice 9 mace, goji berry, bee pollen, aloe, hemp etc.)

Directions:
1. Load your smoothie blender with all the mentioned ingredients and pulse it on high speed for 2 minutes.
2. Pour into a glass and enjoy.

Nutrition Info: (Per Serving): Calories- 390, Fat- 18 g , Protein- 15 g, Carbohydrates- 50 g

Blueberry Peach Smoothie

Servings: 1
Cooking Time: 5 Minutes
Ingredients:
- 1 cup almond milk
- 1 cup peach, cubed (fresh or frozen)
- A handful of blueberries (fresh or frozen)
- 1 cup greens of your choice (kale, spinach)
- 1 tablespoon of Chia seeds
- ½ teaspoon of freshly grated ginger
- 1 tablespoon of any super food of your choice
- 1 tablespoon coconut oil

Directions:
1. Add all the ingredients to the blender jar except the coconut oil and process for 1 minute.
2. Then pour in the oil and blend again for 30 seconds and serve.

Nutrition Info: (Per Serving): Calories- 280, Fat- 18 g, Protein- 3 g, Carbohydrates- 34 g

Ultimate Cold And Flu Fighting Smoothie

Servings: 1
Cooking Time: 5 Minutes
Ingredients:
- 1 large banana, fresh or frozen
- 2 oranges, peeled and chopped

- 2 cups baby spinach
- Freshly squeezed juice of ½ lemon
- 2 tablespoon Chia seeds (soaked)
- 1 teaspoon of freshly grated ginger
- ¼ cup of filtered water

Directions:
1. Whizz all the ingredients in the blender until smooth and serve.

Nutrition Info: (Per Serving): Calories- 330, Fat- 5.8 g, Protein-8 g, Carbohydrates-72 g

Berry Carrot Smoothie

Servings: 1
Cooking Time: 2 Minutes
Ingredients:
- ¾ cup of freshly squeezed orange juice
- ½ cup of low fat plain yogurt
- 1 small carrot, chopped
- 1 cup mixed berries (preferably frozen)
- 2 tablespoon pumpkin seeds

Directions:
1. Just add all the ingredients into your blender jar and process the smoothie until it's nice and frothy.

Nutrition Info: (Per Serving): Calories- 159, Fat- 5 g, Protein- 4 g, Carbohydrates- 25 g

Pomegranate- Berry Smoothie

Servings: 1
Cooking Time: 2 Minutes
Ingredients:
- ¾ cup freshly squeezed pomegranate juice
- 1 cups mixed berries (fresh or frozen)
- 1 cup low fat yogurt
- 2-3 drops of vanilla extract
- 1 teaspoon Chia seeds

Directions:
1. Add all the above ingredients into your blender jar and pulse until thick and frothy.

Nutrition Info: (Per Serving): Calories- 283, Fat-3 g, Protein-7 g, Carbohydrates-58 g

Yogi-berry Smoothie

Servings: 1
Cooking Time: 5 Minutes
Ingredients:
- 2 cups mixed greens of your choice
- 1 cup pineapple, chopped
- ½ orange, peeled and chopped

- 1 kiwi, peeled and chopped
- ½ cup mixed berries (fresh or frozen)
- ½ cup low fat Greek yogurt (plain)
- 1 tablespoon flax seeds (soaked or ground)
- ½ cup filtered water

Directions:
1. To your blender, add all the smoothie ingredients listed above and process until smooth and creamy.

Nutrition Info: (Per Serving): Calories-330, Fat-3.4 g, Protein-18.4 g, Carbohydrates- 162 g

Double Decker Smoothie

Servings: 2
Cooking Time: 10 Minutes
Ingredients:
- For 1st layer (orange):
- 1 persimmon, quartered
- The juice of 1 lime
- 1 cup coconut milk
- 1 mango, peeled and chopped
- 1 tablespoon almond butter
- A pinch of cayenne pepper
- ½ teaspoon turmeric powder
- For 2nd layer (pink)
- 1 small beetroot, peeled and chopped
- 1 cup mixed berries (fresh or frozen)
- ½ cup filtered water
- 1 small grapefruit, peeled and quartered
- 5-6 fresh mint leaves
- Garnish- mint leaves, 1 teaspoon of Chia seeds

Directions:
1. Add the ingredients of the first layer into the blender and process it for 1 minute until smooth.
2. Pour the mixture equally into 2 serving glasses and keep it aside.
3. In the same blender, add the ingredients of the second layer and process whir it up until and smooth.
4. Divide this pink mixture equally into the 2 serving glass, above the first layer.
5. Sprinkle some Chia seeds on top and add a garnish with a mint leaf.
6. Serve immediately.

Nutrition Info: (Per Serving): Calories-320, Fat-5.2 g, Protein-4.5 g, Carbohydrates-72.7 g

Citrus Spinach Immune Booster

Servings: 2
Cooking Time: 5 Minutes
Ingredients:
- 1 orange, peeled, deseeded and chopped

- 1 lime, peeled, deseeded and chopped
- A small handful of spinach leaves, washed
- 1-2 peaches, peeled and chopped
- 2 carrots, peeled and chopped
- 1 ½ cups almond milk (unsweetened)

Directions:
1. Dump all the ingredients into the blender and whip it up until the smoothie is thick and creamy.

Nutrition Info: (Per Serving): Calories-145, Fat-2g, Protein- 4 g, Carbohydrates- 30 g

Berrilicious Chiller

Servings: 2
Cooking Time: 5 Minutes
Ingredients:
- 1 ½ cup mixed berries (fresh or frozen)
- 1 tablespoon freshly squeezed lemon juice
- 6 ounces of unsweetened almond milk
- 2 teaspoons of freshly grated ginger
- 1 tablespoon flax seeds
- 1 ½ tablespoons of raw organic honey
- A handful of ice cubes

Directions:
1. Add all the ingredients into your blender and process until smooth and frothy.
2. Serve and enjoy immediately.

Nutrition Info: (Per Serving): Calories- 110, Fat-1.5 g, Protein- 1 g, Carbs-26 g

DETOX AND CLEANSE SMOOTHIES

Cacao Cantaloupe Smoothie

Servings: 2
Cooking Time: 5 Minutes
Ingredients:
- 1 cup unsweetened almond milk
- 1 cup whole strawberries (fresh or frozen)
- 1 cup cantaloupe, chopped
- 1 banana, chopped (fresh or frozen)
- 2-3 fresh chard leaves
- 1 tablespoon cacao powder
- 1 tablespoon Chia seeds, Soaked

Directions:
1. Add all the ingredients into your blender and process on medium high speed for 45 seconds or until done.

Nutrition Info: (Per Serving): Calories- 330, Fat- 0 g, Protein- 10 g, Carbohydrates- 61 g

Lime And Lemon Detox Punch

Servings: 2
Cooking Time: 5 Minutes
Ingredients:
- 1 banana, chopped (fresh or frozen)
- ½ cup blueberries (fresh or frozen)
- 1 cup fresh kale stems chopped off
- ½ sweet lime, peeled, de-seeded and chopped
- 1 tablespoon freshly squeezed Lemon juice
- ½ tablespoon freshly grated ginger
- 1 cup filtered water
- 1 teaspoon raw organic honey
- A pinch of Celtic salt

Directions:
1. Place all the ingredients into your blender and puree it on medium high until the smoothie is thick and frothy.

Nutrition Info: (Per Serving): Calories- 190, Fat- 1 g, Protein- 3 g, Carbohydrates- 51 g

Pineapple Coconut Detox Smoothie

Servings: 2
Cooking Time: 10 Minutes
Ingredients:
- 4 cups kale, chopped
- 2 cups of coconut water
- 2 bananas
- 2 cups pineapple

Directions:

1. Add all the listed ingredients to a blender
2. Blend until you have a smooth and creamy texture
3. Serve chilled and enjoy!

Nutrition Info: Calories: 299; Fat: 1.1g; Carbohydrates: 71.5g; Protein: 7.9g

Apple And Green Slush

Servings: 1
Cooking Time: 2 Minutes
Ingredients:
- 1 granny smith apple, cored and chopped
- 1 large, ripe banana, chopped (fresh or frozen)
- ½ cup Italian flat leaf parsley
- 1 cup collard greens (stems removed)
- 1 teaspoon freshly squeezed lemon juice
- A few cubes of ice

Directions:
1. Add all the ingredients to your blender and blend until smooth.

Nutrition Info: (Per Serving): Calories- 105, Fat- 0 g, Protein- 2 g, Carbohydrates-26 g

Lemon-lettuce Cooler

Servings: 2
Cooking Time: 5 Minutes
Ingredients:
- 1 green cucumber, deseeded and chopped
- 1 green apple, cored and quartered
- A handful of romaine lettuce, chopped
- 1 small head of broccoli, chopped
- A handful of kale stems re moved
- 3-4 celery stalk, chopped
- 1 teaspoon freshly squeezed lemon juice
- 3-4 ice cubes (optional)

Directions:
1. Combine all the ingredients in your blender and whizz it on high for 30 seconds.

Nutrition Info: (Per Serving): Calories- 128, Fat- 0 g, Protein- 7.2 g, Carbohydrates- 49 g

Papaya Berry Banana Blend

Servings: 2
Cooking Time: 5 Minutes
Ingredients:
- 1 cup, homemade, unsweetened almond milk
- 1 ½ cup papaya, peeled and chopped
- 1 large banana, chopped (fresh or frozen)
- A handful of fresh strawberries

- 1 large pitted peach

Directions:
1. Add the fruits and almond milk into the blender and puree until thick and creamy.

Nutrition Info: (Per Serving): Calories- 318, Fat- 3 g, Protein- 5 g, Carbohydrates- 70 g

Blueberry Detox Drink

Servings: 2
Cooking Time: 5 Minutes
Ingredients:
- 1 cup ice
- 2 tablespoons spirulina
- ½ frozen banana, sliced
- 2 cups blueberries, frozen
- 2 cups baby spinach
- 2 cups coconut water

Directions:
1. Add all the ingredients except vegetables/fruits first
2. Blend until smooth
3. Add the vegetable/fruits
4. Blend until smooth
5. Add a few ice cubes and serve the smoothie
6. Enjoy!

Nutrition Info: Calories: 685; Fat: 60g; Carbohydrates: 40g; Protein: 32g

Mango Pepper Smoothie

Servings: 2
Cooking Time: 5 Minutes
Ingredients:
- 2 cups fresh coconut water
- 2 cups mango, peeled and chopped
- ¼ cup freshly squeezed lime juice
- A pinch of cayenne pepper
- 1-2 cubes of ice

Directions:
1. Place all the ingredients into the blender and pulse on high for 30 seconds or until the smoothie has reached your desired consistency.

Nutrition Info: (Per Serving): Calories-160, Fat- 0 g, Protein- 3 g, Carbohydrates- 40 g

Apple And Pear Detox Wonder

Servings: 2
Cooking Time: 5 Minutes
Ingredients:
- 1 apple, cored and chopped
- 1 pear, cored and chopped

- 1 cup kale leaves, washed and stems removed
- 1 cup dandelion greens, washed
- ½ cup arugula, washed
- 1/2 cup freshly squeezed lemon juice
- 1 cup filtered water
- ½ teaspoon freshly grated ginger
- ½ teaspoon of cayenne pepper powder
- 1 teaspoon of raw organic honey (optional)
- 1 teaspoon Maca powder

Directions:
1. Load your blender with all the above ingredients and blend until rich and creamy.

Nutrition Info: (Per Serving): Calories- 260, Fat- 2 g, Protein- 4 g, Carbohydrates- 67 g

Strawberry-beet Smoothie

Servings: 2 Large
Cooking Time: 5 Minutes
Ingredients:
- 1 cup unsweetened almond milk
- 1 cup red beet, peeled and chopped
- 1 orange, peeled and chopped
- 3 cups baby spinach, washed
- 1 banana, chopped (fresh or frozen)
- 1 cup strawberries (fresh or frozen)

Directions:
1. Place all the ingredients in your blender jar and blend for 1-2 minutes until smooth.

Nutrition Info: (Per Serving): Calories- 333, Fat- 4 g, Proteins- 9 g, Carbohydrates- 71 g

Green Tea- Berry Smoothie

Servings: 2
Cooking Time: 10 Minutes
Ingredients:
- 1 cup green tea (chilled)
- 1/3 cup raspberries (fresh or frozen)
- 1/3 cup blueberries (fresh or frozen)
- 1/3 cup black berries (fresh or frozen)
- ½ small avocado, peeled and chopped
- 1 cup fresh spinach, washed
- 1/3 cup plain yogurt
- 2 teaspoon of freshly squeezed lemon juice

Directions:
1. First, prepare a cup green tea as usual (sugarless) and let it cool down at room temperature.
2. Then chill it in the refrigerator for a few minutes.
3. After the tea has chilled, pour all the ingredients into the blender jar and whizz it for 1 minute or until the smoothie is thick and creamy.

Nutrition Info: (Per Serving): Calories- 365. Fat- 15 g, Protein-10 g, Carbohydrates- 56.6 g

Pear Jicama Detox Smoothie

Servings: 2
Cooking Time: 10 Minutes
Ingredients:
- 3 tablespoons red kale
- 8 tablespoons jicama, peeled and chopped
- 1 lemon, juiced
- 1 pear, chopped
- 1 teaspoon reishi mushroom
- 1 tablespoon flaxseed
- 1 cup of water
- 1 cup ice

Directions:
1. Add all the listed ingredients to a blender
2. Blend until smooth
3. Serve chilled and enjoy!

Nutrition Info: Calories: 102; Fat: 0g; Carbohydrates: 24g; Protein: 2g

Punchy Watermelon

Servings: 2
Cooking Time: 5 Minutes
Ingredients:
- 1 large cucumber, cubed
- 1 cup kale, chopped
- 1 cup baby spinach, chopped
- 4 cups watermelon, chopped

Directions:
1. Add all the ingredients except vegetables/fruits first
2. Blend until smooth
3. Add the vegetable/fruits
4. Blend until smooth
5. Add a few ice cubes and serve the smoothie
6. Enjoy!

Nutrition Info: Calories: 464; Fat: 20g; Carbohydrates: 65g; Protein: 23g

A Melon Cucumber Medley

Servings: 2
Cooking Time: 5 Minutes
Ingredients:
- ¾ cup honeydew melon, peeled and chopped
- 2 cups kale, chopped
- 1 medium cucumber, cubed

Directions:

1. Add all the ingredients except vegetables/fruits first
2. Blend until smooth
3. Add the vegetable/fruits
4. Blend until smooth
5. Add a few ice cubes and serve the smoothie
6. Enjoy!

Nutrition Info: Calories: 112; Fat: 2g; Carbohydrates: 30g; Protein: 2g

PROTEIN SMOOTHIES

Dark Chocolate Peppermint Smoothie

Servings: 2
Cooking Time: 10 Minutes
Ingredients:
- 2 large bananas, frozen
- 2 scoops chocolate protein powder
- 4 tablespoons cocoa powder
- 2 cups almond milk
- 2 pinches sea salt
- ½ teaspoon peppermint extract
- 4 large ice cubes
- 1 tablespoon dark chocolate chips for garnishing

Directions:
1. Add all the listed ingredients to a blender
2. Blend until you have a smooth and creamy texture
3. Serve chilled and enjoy!

Nutrition Info: Calories: 132; Fat: 2.6g; Carbohydrates: 23.8g; Protein: 7.2g

Mango Mania

Servings: 2
Cooking Time: 2 Minutes
Ingredients:
- 1 large cup mango, peeled and chopped
- 2 teaspoons help hearts
- ¾ cup freshly prepared apple juice
- 1 tablespoons goji berries
- ½ teaspoon chili powder
- 1 tablespoon freshly squeezed lemon juice
- 1 tablespoon freshly squeezed lime juice
- ½ cup filtered water
- 1 teaspoon raw organic honey
- 2-3 ice cubes (optional)

Directions:
1. Place all the above ingredients into the blender jar and process until the mixture is thick and creamy.

Nutrition Info: (Per Serving): Calories- 325, Fat- 8 g, Protein- 6 g, Carbohydrates- 61 g

Spiced Up Banana Shake

Servings: 2
Cooking Time: 5 Minutes
Ingredients:
- 2 scoops vanilla protein powder
- ½ teaspoon ground cinnamon

- 1/8 teaspoon ground nutmeg
- 2 ripe bananas
- 12 ice cubes

Directions:
1. Add all the ingredients except vegetables/fruits first
2. Blend until smooth
3. Add the vegetable/fruits
4. Blend until smooth
5. Add a few ice cubes and serve the smoothie
6. Enjoy!

Nutrition Info: Calories: 506; Fat: 30g; Carbohydrates: 56g; Protein: 12g

Subtle Raspberry Smoothie

Servings: 1
Cooking Time: 10 Minutes
Ingredients:
- ½ cup raspberries
- 1 scoop vanilla whey protein powder
- 1 scoop prebiotic fiber
- 1 cup unsweetened almond milk, vanilla
- 2 tablespoons coconut oil
- ¼ cup coconut flakes, unsweetened
- 3-4 ice cubes

Directions:
1. Add all the listed ingredients into your blender
2. Blend until smooth
3. Serve chilled and enjoy!

Nutrition Info: Calories: 258; Fat: 22g; Carbohydrates: 7g; Protein: 14g

Strawberry Coconut Snowflake

Servings: 2
Cooking Time: 2 Minutes
Ingredients:
- ½ unsweetened, fresh coconut milk
- 1 cup whole strawberries (fresh or frozen)
- ½ cup plain low fat Greek yogurt
- ¼ cup freshly squeezed orange
- ½ teaspoon raw organic honey
- 2-3 ice cubes

Directions:
1. Just place all the ingredients into the blender and pulse until smooth. Serve immediately!

Nutrition Info: (Per Serving): Calories- 160, Fat- 2.8 g, Protein- 12 g, Carbohydrates- 24 g

Ginger Plum Punch

Servings: 4
Cooking Time: 5 Minutes
Ingredients:

- 1 ½ cups tofu
- ½ cup unsweetened almond milk
- 1 cup whole strawberries (fresh or frozen)
- 1 cup whole raspberries (fresh or frozen)
- ¼ cup Goji berries
- ¼ cup whole almonds
- ½ teaspoon vanilla extract
- 1 teaspoon freshly grated ginger
- 1-2 teaspoons raw organic honey
- 8-10 mint leaves
- 4-5 ice cubes

Directions:
1. Place all the ingredients into the blender, secure the lid and whizz on medium high for 30 seconds or until done. Serve immediately.

Nutrition Info: (Per Serving): Calories- 240, Fat- 6.8 g, Protein- 15 g, Carbohydrates- 33g

Peppermint And Dark Chocolate Shake Delight

Servings: 2
Cooking Time: 5 Minutes
Ingredients:

- ¼ teaspoon peppermint extract
- 1 scoop chocolate whey protein powder
- 2 tablespoons cocoa powder
- Pinch of salt
- 1 cup almond milk
- 1 large frozen banana
- 2-3 large ice cubes

Directions:
1. Add all the ingredients except vegetables/fruits first
2. Blend until smooth
3. Add the vegetable/fruits
4. Blend until smooth
5. Add a few ice cubes and serve the smoothie
6. Enjoy!

Nutrition Info: Calories: 374; Fat: 26g; Carbohydrates: 26g; Protein: 16g

Mad Mocha Glass

Servings: 2
Cooking Time: 5 Minutes
Ingredients:

- 4 ice cubes
- 1 scoop 100% chocolate whey protein
- ½ scoop vanilla protein powder
- 6 ounces water
- 6 ounces cold coffee

Directions:
1. Add all the ingredients except vegetables/fruits first
2. Blend until smooth
3. Add the vegetable/fruits
4. Blend until smooth
5. Add a few ice cubes and serve the smoothie
6. Enjoy!

Nutrition Info: Calories: 306; Fat: 4g; Carbohydrates: 43g; Protein: 28g

Strawberry Quick Protein Smoothie

Servings: 3-4
Cooking Time: 5 Minutes
Ingredients:
- 2 cups unsweetened almond milk
- 2 cups whole strawberries (fresh or frozen)
- 2/4 cup low fat cottage cheese or silken tofu
- 1 teaspoon vanilla extract
- 1 teaspoon raw organic honey
- 1-2 ice cubes (optional)

Directions:
1. Whizz all the ingredients in the blender until smooth and serve.

Nutrition Info: (Per Serving): Calories-166, Fat- 5 g, Protein- 12 g, Carbohydrates-19 g

Mixed Berry Melba

Servings: 3
Cooking Time: 5 Minutes
Ingredients:
- 1 cup low fat plain yogurt
- ½ cup mixed berries (fresh or frozen)
- ½ cup whole strawberries (fresh or frozen)
- 1 small banana, chopped
- 3 teaspoons peanut butter or peanut powder
- 2 teaspoons chia seeds
- 1 teaspoon flaxseeds
- ¼ cup filtered water
- 1-2 ice cubes (optional)

Directions:
1. Dump all the ingredients into the blender and whip it up until the smoothie is thick and creamy.

Nutrition Info: (Per Serving): Calories- 340, Fat- 6.3 g, Protein- 25 g, Carbohydrates- 52 g

Berry Dreamsicle Smoothie

Servings: 3 - 4
Cooking Time: 5 Minutes
Ingredients:
- 1 cup whole blueberries (fresh or frozen)
- 1/2 ripe banana, chopped
- ½ cup whole strawberries (fresh or frozen)
- 3 large handfuls of chopped lucent kale
- 1 tablespoon freshly squeezed lemon juice
- 2 tablespoons chia seeds
- ½ cup filtered water
- 3-4 ice cubes

Directions:
1. Whizz all the ingredients in the blender until smooth and serve.

Nutrition Info: (Per Serving): Calories- 400, Fat- 10.5 g, Protein- 17 g, Carbohydrates- 70 g

Green Protein Smoothie

Servings: 2
Cooking Time: 10 Minutes
Ingredients:
- 2 bananas
- 4 cups mixed greens
- 2 tablespoons almond butter
- 1 cup almond milk, unsweetened

Directions:
1. Add all the listed ingredients to a blender
2. Blend until you have a smooth and creamy texture
3. Serve chilled and enjoy!

Nutrition Info: Calories: 230; Fat: 5.8g; Carbohydrates: 39.5g; Protein: 7.8g

Berry Orange Madness

Servings: 2-3
Cooking Time: 2 Minutes
Ingredients:
- 1 cup mixed berries (fresh or frozen)
- 1 large orange, peeled, seeded and segmented
- 1 cup low fat plain yogurt
- 1 banana, chopped (frozen)
- ¼ teaspoon vanilla extract
- 1-2 ice cubes

Directions:
1. Pour all the ingredients into your blender and process until smooth.

Nutrition Info: (Per Serving): Calories-210, Fat-2 g, Protein- 8.3 g, Carbohydrates- 40 g

The Cacao Super Smoothie

Servings: 1
Cooking Time: 10 Minutes
Ingredients:
- ½ avocado, peeled, pitted, sliced
- ½ cup frozen blueberries, unsweetened
- ½ cup almond milk, vanilla, unsweetened
- ½ cup half and half
- 1 scoop whey vanilla protein powder
- 1 tablespoon cacao powder
- Liquid stevia

Directions:
1. Add listed ingredients to a blender
2. Blend until you get a smooth and creamy texture
3. Serve chilled and enjoy!

Nutrition Info: Calories: 445; Fat: 14g; Carbohydrates: 9g; Protein: 16g

WEIGHT LOSS SMOOTHIES

Meanie-greenie Weigh Loss Smoothie

Servings: 2-3
Cooking Time: 5 Minutes
Ingredients:
- 1 cup kale, stems removed
- 1 cup green cucumber, de-seeded and chopped
- 1 celery stalk, chopped
- 1 small pear, peeled, cored and chopped
- 1 teaspoon freshly grated ginger
- A handful of parsley
- 1 ½ cups of filtered water
- 1 teaspoon freshly squeezed lemon juice

Directions:
1. Place all the ingredients in the order listed above and pulse until the desired consistency is attained.

Nutrition Info: (Per Serving): Calories- 64.3, Fat- 0.3 g, Protein- 1 g, Carbohydrates- 15.8 g

The Fat Burner Espresso Smoothie

Servings: 2
Cooking Time: 10 Minutes
Ingredients:
- ¼ cup Greek yogurt, full fat
- 1 scoop Isopure Zero Carb protein powder
- 1 espresso shot
- 5 ice cubes
- Liquid stevia to sweeten
- Pinch of cinnamon

Directions:
1. Add listed ingredients to a blender
2. Blend until you have a smooth and creamy texture
3. Serve chilled and enjoy!

Nutrition Info: Calories: 270; Fat: 16g; Carbohydrates: 2g; Protein: 30g

Green Tea- Mango Smoothie

Servings: 2
Cooking Time: 10 Minutes
Ingredients:
- 1 cup mango, chopped (fresh or frozen)
- 1 cup green tea
- 1 cup fresh spinach, chopped
- ½ cup avocado, chopped
- 1 teaspoon coconut oil
- ½ teaspoon raw organic honey

- A inch of Celtic salt

Directions:
1. First, prepare a cup of your favorite green tea and allow w it to cool to room temperature.
2. Once the tea has cooled, combine all the ingredients in the high speed blender and whizz until thick and creamy.
3. Serve and enjoy!

Nutrition Info: (Per Serving): Calories-330, Fat- 21 g, Protein- 4g, Carbohydrates- 35 g

Spinach, Carrot And Tomato Smoothie

Servings: 2
Cooking Time: 2 Minutes
Ingredients:
- 1 cup fresh spinach, chopped
- 1-2 celery stalks chopped
- 1 small carrot, peeled and chopped
- 1 large tomato, chopped
- 1 small bell pepper, deseeded and chopped
- ¼ small onion
- 3-4 sprigs of cilantro leaves, chopped
- ½ sweet lime, Peeled and deseeded
- 1 ¼ cup of filtered water

Directions:
1. Place everything into the blender and run it on high for 30 seconds. Pour into serving glasses and enjoy.

Nutrition Info: (Per Serving): Calories- 74, Fat- 0.8 g, Protein- 3.5 g, Carbohydrates- 16.5 g

Tropical Avocado Smoothie

Servings: 3
Cooking Time: 5 Minutes
Ingredients:
- 1 ½ cups whole strawberries (fresh r frozen)
- ¾ cup organic coconut milk
- 1 ½ cup mango, chopped
- 1 ½ cups freshly squeezed pineapple juice
- 1/3 cup avocado, chopped
- 2 kiwi fruits, peeled and chopped

Directions:
1. Place all the ingredients into your blender and run it on high for 20 seconds or until done.

Nutrition Info: (Per Serving): Calories- 185, Fat- 6 g, Protein- 2.2 g, Carbohydrates- 33 g

Carrot Coconut Smoothie

Servings: 2
Cooking Time: 5 Minutes
Ingredients:

- 6 ounces carrots, chopped
- 1 orange, peeled
- 4 ounces pineapple
- 1 teaspoon Camu Camu
- 2 tablespoons coconut flakes
- 1 cup ice
- 1 cup of water

Directions:
1. Add all the listed ingredients to a blender
2. Blend until you have a smooth and creamy texture
3. Serve chilled and enjoy!

Nutrition Info: Calories: 140; Fat: 2g; Carbohydrates: 29g; Protein: 2g

Zucchini Apple Smoothie

Servings: 2
Cooking Time: 5 Minutes
Ingredients:
- 1½ cups crushed ice
- 1 tablespoon Spirulina
- 1 lemon, juiced
- 1 stalk celery
- ¾ avocado
- 2 apples, quartered
- ½ cup zucchini, diced

Directions:
1. Add all the ingredients except vegetables/fruits first
2. Blend until smooth
3. Add the vegetable/fruits
4. Blend until smooth
5. Add a few ice cubes and serve the smoothie
6. Enjoy!

Nutrition Info: Calories: 80; Fat: 4g; Carbohydrates: 11g; Protein: 2g

Carrot Spice Smoothie

Servings: 2
Cooking Time: 5 Minutes
Ingredients:
- 1 cup unsweetened almond milk
- 1 ripe banana, chopped
- 1 cup carrots, peeled and chopped
- 4 ounces plain yogurt
- 1 tablespoon raw organic honey
- ¼ teaspoon freshly grated ginger
- ¼ teaspoon cinnamon powder
- A pinch of nutmeg powder

- 3-4 ice cubes

Directions:
1. Add all the ingredients into the blender one by one and pulse until thick and creamy.

Nutrition Info: (Per Serving): Calories- 295, Fat- 3.5 g, Protein- 9 g, Carbohydrates- 61.5 g

Kale Strawberry Smoothie

Servings: 2
Cooking Time: 10 Minutes
Ingredients:
- 2 cups kale, chopped
- 2 bananas
- 2 cups strawberries
- 2 cups ice
- 2 cups yogurt

Directions:
1. Add all the listed ingredients to a blender
2. Blend until you have a smooth and creamy texture
3. Serve chilled and enjoy!

Nutrition Info: Calories: 358; Fat: 3.8g; Carbohydrates: 62.3g; Protein: 18.2g

Cucumber Kale And Lime Apple Smoothie

Servings: 2
Cooking Time: 5 Minutes
Ingredients:
- 1 cup crushed ice
- 1 cucumber, diced
- ¼ cup raspberries, chopped
- 1 lime, juiced
- 1 avocado, diced
- 2 apples, quartered
- 1 cup kale, chopped

Directions:
1. Add all the ingredients except vegetables/fruits first
2. Blend until smooth
3. Add the vegetable/fruits
4. Blend until smooth
5. Add a few ice cubes and serve the smoothie
6. Enjoy!

Nutrition Info: Calories: 291; Fat: 2g; Carbohydrates: 38g; Protein: 7g

A-b-c Smoothie

Servings: 1-2
Cooking Time: 2 Minutes
Ingredients:

- 1 cup unsweetened almond milk
- 2 large bananas (fresh or frozen)
- 1 teaspoon Chia seeds, soaked
- 1 tablespoon almond butter
- 1 teaspoon vanilla extract
- 1 teaspoon pomegranate seeds for garnish

Directions:
1. To your blender, add all the items and process until you get a thick and creamy smoothie.
2. Pour into a glass and enjoy.

Nutrition Info: (Per Serving): Calories- 184, Fat- 6.6 g, Protein- 3.6 g, Carbohydrates- 30 g

Peanut Butter Berry Smoothie

Servings: 2
Cooking Time: 2 Minutes
Ingredients:
- 1 tablespoon peanut butter
- 2 cups strawberry (fresh or frozen)
- 1 large banana, chopped (fresh or frozen)
- ½ cup plain or Greek yogurt
- A handful of ice cubes

Directions:
1. Add all the ingredients into the blender and whip it up until smooth and nice.
2. Pour into cool serving glasses and enjoy.

Nutrition Info: (Per Serving): Calories- 327, Fat- 7 g, Protein- 18 g, Carbohydrates- 55 g

Apple And Zucchini Medley

Servings: 2
Cooking Time: 5 Minutes
Ingredients:
- 1 cup crushed ice
- 1 jalapeno pepper
- 2 stalks celery, diced
- ¾ avocado, cubed
- 2 apples, quartered

Directions:
1. Add all the ingredients except vegetables/fruits first
2. Blend until smooth
3. Add the vegetable/fruits
4. Blend until smooth
5. Add a few ice cubes and serve the smoothie
6. Enjoy!

Nutrition Info: Calories: 282; Fat: 2g; Carbohydrates: 62g; Protein: 4g

Banana, Almond, And Dark Chocolate Smoothie

Servings: 2

Cooking Time: 5 Minutes

Ingredients:

- 1 cup banana, sliced
- 4 tablespoons dark chocolate, grated 80% cocoa
- 8 almonds, soaked overnight
- ½ cup milk, low-fat and chilled

Directions:

1. Toss the sliced bananas, grated dark chocolate, almonds, and chilled milk
2. Add all the listed ingredients to a blender
3. Blend until you have a smooth and creamy texture
4. Serve chilled and enjoy!

Nutrition Info: Calories: 114; Fat: 1g; Carbohydrates: 22g; Protein: 5g

KID FRIENDLY HEALTHY SMOOTHIES

Pina- Banana Quickie

Servings: 2
Cooking Time: 5 Minutes
Ingredients:
- 1 cup plain unsweetened soy milk or almond milk
- 1 small ripe banana, chopped (fresh or frozen)
- 1 cup pineapple, peeled and chopped
- 1 teaspoon flaxseeds
- 3-4 ice cubes

Directions:
1. Add all the ingredients into the high speed blender and whizz until smooth.

Nutrition Info: (Per Serving): Calories- 213, Fat- 4.8 g, Protein- 8 g, Carbohydrates- 35 g

Delish Pineapple And Coconut Milk Smoothie

Servings: 2
Cooking Time: 5 Minutes
Ingredients:
- ¾ cup of coconut water
- ¼ cup pineapple, frozen

Directions:
1. Add listed ingredients to a blender
2. Blend on high until you have a smooth and creamy texture
3. Serve chilled and enjoy!

Nutrition Info: Calories: 132; Fat: 12g; Carbohydrates: 7g; Protein: 1g

Nutella Lovers Smoothie

Servings: 4
Cooking Time: 10 Minutes
Ingredients:
- 2 cups pear, ripped and chopped
- ½ cup roasted, unsalted hazelnuts
- 3 cups of coconut water
- 4 tablespoons cocoa powder, unsalted
- 4 Medjool dates pitted
- 3 teaspoons vanilla extract
- 4 cups ice

Directions:
1. Add all the listed ingredients to a blender
2. Blend until you have a smooth and creamy texture
3. Serve chilled and enjoy!

Nutrition Info: Calories: 301; Fat: 6.9g; Carbohydrates: 59.8g; Protein: 5g

Raw Chocolate Smoothie

Servings: 2
Cooking Time: 10 Minutes
Ingredients:
- 2 medium bananas
- 4 tablespoons peanut butter, raw
- 1 cup almond milk
- 3 tablespoons cocoa powder, raw
- 2 tablespoons honey, raw

Directions:
1. Add all the listed ingredients to a blender
2. Blend until you have a smooth and creamy texture
3. Serve chilled and enjoy!

Nutrition Info: Calories: 217; Fat: 2.8g; Carbohydrates: 52.7g; Protein: 3.4g

Mixed Fruit Madness

Servings: 1
Cooking Time: 10 Minutes
Ingredients:
- 1 cup spring mix salad blend
- 2 cups water
- 3 medium blackberries, whole
- 1 packet Stevia, optional
- 1 tablespoon avocado oil
- 1 tablespoon coconut flakes shredded and unsweetened
- 2 tablespoons pecans, chopped
- 1 tablespoon hemp seeds
- 1 tablespoon sunflower seeds

Directions:
1. Add all the ingredients except vegetables/fruits first
2. Blend until smooth
3. Add the vegetable/fruits
4. Blend until smooth
5. Add a few ice cubes and serve the smoothie
6. Enjoy!

Nutrition Info: Calories: 150; Fat: 2g; Carbohydrates: 37g; Protein: 3g

Berry Peachy Blush

Servings: 3
Cooking Time: 2 Minutes
Ingredients:
- 1 cup fresh, unsweetened coconut milk
- 1 cup whole strawberries (fresh or frozen)
- ¾ cup peaches, pitted (fresh or frozen)
- A small ripe banana, chopped

- 3 teaspoons raw organic honey
- ¼ cup filtered water
- 4-5 ice cubes

Directions:

1. Place all the above ingredients into the blender jar and process until the mixture is thick and creamy.

Nutrition Info: (Per Serving): Calories- 385, Fat-20 g, Protein- 4.2 g, Carbohydrates- 51 g

Peanut Butter Broccoli Smoothie

Servings: 3
Cooking Time: 5 Minutes

Ingredients:

- 1 cup unsweetened almond milk
- 1 cup fresh spinach, washed and chopped
- 1 cup broccoli florets, washed and chopped
- 1 large kale leaf, washed and chopped
- 1 ripe banana, chopped
- 2 teaspoons peanut butter
- 1 teaspoon raw organic honey (optional)

Directions:

1. Add all the ingredients into the high speed blender and whizz until smooth.

Nutrition Info: (Per Serving): Calories- 325, Fat- 14 g, Protein- 10 g, Carbohydrates- 46 g

Beet Berry Chiller

Servings: 2
Cooking Time: 2 Minutes

Ingredients:

- ¾ cup freshly prepared cranberry juice (unsweetened)
- A small handful of cranberries (fresh or frozen)
- 1 cup raw beet, peeled and chopped
- 4-5 whole strawberries (fresh or frozen)
- 1 tablespoon raw organic honey
- 2 teaspoons freshly squeezed lemon juice
- 4- ice cubes

Directions:

1. Pour all the ingredients into your blender jar and process until smooth.

Nutrition Info: (Per Serving): Calories- 90, Fat- 0 g, Protein- 1.2 g, Carbohydrates- 22 g

Cool Coco-loco Cream Shake

Servings: 1
Cooking Time: 10 Minutes

Ingredients:

- ½ cup coconut milk

- 2 tablespoons Dutch-processed cocoa powder, unsweetened
- 1 cup brewed coffee, chilled
- 1-2 packs stevia
- 1 tablespoon hemp seeds

Directions:
1. Add all the ingredients except vegetables/fruits first
2. Blend until smooth
3. Add the vegetable/fruits
4. Blend until smooth
5. Add a few ice cubes and serve the smoothie
6. Enjoy!

Nutrition Info: Calories: 337; Fat: 11g; Carbohydrates: 38g; Protein: 1g

Delicious Creamy Choco Shake

Servings: 1
Cooking Time: 10 Minutes
Ingredients:
- ½ cup heavy cream
- 2 tablespoons cocoa powder
- 1 pack stevia
- 1 cup water

Directions:
1. Add all the ingredients except vegetables/fruits first
2. Blend until smooth
3. Add the vegetable/fruits
4. Blend until smooth
5. Add a few ice cubes and serve the smoothie
6. Enjoy!

Nutrition Info: Calories: 180; Fat: 6g; Carbohydrates: 30g; Protein: 3g

Salad Smoothie

Servings: 4
Cooking Time: 5 Minutes
Ingredients:
- ½ cup unsweetened almond milk or soy milk
- 1 small orange, peeled and seeded
- ½ cup broccoli florets, washed
- 1 cup whole strawberries (fresh or frozen)
- A small handful of baby spinach, washed and chopped
- 1 small ripe banana, chopped
- 1 small peach, pitted and chopped
- ½ cup pineapple, peeled and chopped
- ¼ cup carrot, peeled and chopped
- A handful of grapes, seedless (red or green)
- 2 tablespoon freshly squeezed lemon juice

- 4-5 ice cubes

Directions:
1. Whizz all the ingredients in the blender until smooth and serve.

Nutrition Info: (Per Serving): Calories- 118, Fat-1.2 g, Protein-3.2 g, Carbohydrates- 28 g

Banana-cado Smoothie

Servings: 3
Cooking Time: 5 Minutes
Ingredients:
- 1 cup fresh organic coconut water
- ½ cup unsweetened almond milk
- ½ cup unsweetened coconut milk
- 1 ripe banana, chopped
- 2 teaspoons chia sees
- 2 tablespoons fresh avocado flesh

Directions:
1. Place all the above ingredients into the blender jar and process until the mixture is thick and creamy.

Nutrition Info: (Per Serving): Calories- 465, Fat- 7 g, Protein- 7 g, Carbohydrates- 13 g

Peanut Butter Jelly Smoothie

Servings: 2
Cooking Time: 2 Minutes
Ingredients:
- 1 cup whole raspberries (fresh or frozen)
- 2 teaspoons peanut butter
- ½ large banana, chopped
- 1 cup unsweetened almond milk
- ½ teaspoon raw organic honey
- 2-3 ice cubes

Directions:
1. Pour all the ingredients into your blender and process until smooth.

Nutrition Info: (Per Serving): Calories-270, Fat- 12 g, Protein- 7 g, Carbohydrates- 40 g

Berry Almond Breakfast Blend

Servings: 2
Cooking Time: 2 Minutes
Ingredients:
- ½ cup fresh butter milk
- ½ cup plain low fat yogurt
- ¼ cup fresh raspberries
- ¼ cup seedless red grapes
- 1 small ripe banana, chopped

- ½ cup blueberries (fresh or frozen)
- 2 teaspoons rolled oats
- 1 teaspoon flaxseed powder
- 1/4 cup almonds

Directions:
1. Blend all the ingredients into the blender and enjoy!

Nutrition Info: (Per Serving): Calories-260, Fat- 6.2 g, Protein- 8.9 g, Carbohydrates- 45 g

HEART HEALTHY SMOOTHIES

Spinach And Grape Smoothie

Servings: 1 Large
Cooking Time: 5 Minutes
Ingredients:
- 1 cup red grapes (seedless)
- 2 cups baby spinach
- 1 banana (fresh or frozen)
- 1 tablespoon Chia seeds (soaked)
- 1 teaspoon freshly squeezed lemon juice
- A handful of ice cubes

Directions:
1. Load all the ingredients into your blender jar and secure it tightly with a lid.
2. Pulse it on medium speed for 30 seconds and on high for 1 minute or until smooth.

Nutrition Info: (Per Serving): Calories-107, Fat-2.4 g, Protein-1.5 g, Carbohydrates-26.5 g

Peach-ban-illa Smoothie

Servings: 2 Small
Cooking Time: 5 Minutes
Ingredients:
- 1 ¼ cup peaches, pitted and chopped
- 1 large banana (fresh or frozen)
- 1 cup plain yogurt
- 1 teaspoon vanilla extract
- 1 teaspoon Chia seeds, soaked
- A handful of ice

Directions:
1. Combine all the ingredients in the blender and blend until the desired consistency is got.

Nutrition Info: (Per Serving): Calories- 170, Fat- 2 g, Protein- 5 g, Carbohydrates- 45 g

Chia-cacao Melon Smoothie

Servings: 2
Cooking Time: 5 Minutes
Ingredients:
- 1 cup fresh strawberries
- 1 cup cantaloupe, chopped
- 1 large banana (fresh or frozen)
- 2 large chard leaves, chopped
- 1 cup unsweetened almond milk
- 1 tablespoon cacao powder
- 1 tablespoons Chia seeds, soaked

Directions:
1. Pour all the ingredients into your blender and whizz it up on high speed for 45 seconds or until done.

Nutrition Info: (Per Serving): Calories- 330, Fat- 0 g, Protein- 11 g, Carbohydrates- 62 g

Almond- Citrus Punch

Servings: 2
Cooking Time: 2 Minutes
Ingredients:
- 1 cup unsweetened almond milk
- ½ cup freshly squeezed orange juice
- 1 tablespoon raw organic honey
- 1/3 cup freshly squeezed lime juice
- 1 tablespoon freshly squeezed lemon
- ¼ teaspoon vanilla extract
- A handful of ice cubes

Directions:
1. Pour all the ingredients into the blender and blend for 45 seconds until well combined.

Nutrition Info: (Per Serving): Calories- 150, Fat- 4 g, Protein- 2 g, Carbohydrates- 30 g

Almond-banana Blend

Servings: 3
Cooking Time: 5 Minutes
Ingredients:
- 4 large, ripe bananas (fresh or frozen)
- 1 cup unsweetened almond milk
- 2 tablespoons almonds (soaked and chopped)
- 1 cup plain yogurt
- 3 teaspoons raw organic honey

Directions:
1. Pour all the ingredients into the blender and puree until a creamy smoothie is got.

Nutrition Info: (Per Serving): Calories- 192, Fat- 5 g, Protein- 5 g, Carbohydrates- 38 g

Pina Berry Smoothie

Servings: 2
Cooking Time: 2 Minutes
Ingredients:
- 1 cup whole strawberries (fresh or frozen)
- 1 cup pineapple, chopped fresh or frozen)
- 1 teaspoon vanilla extract
- 1 cup plain yogurt
- 4-5 ice cubes

Directions:
1. Pour everything into the blender and blend until thick and frothy.

Nutrition Info: (Per Serving): Calories: 12, Fat-0.5 g, Protein-6 g, Carbohydrates-25 g

Beet And Apple Smoothie

Servings: 2
Cooking Time: 5 Minutes
Ingredients:
- 2 beetroots, peeled and chopped
- ½ cup blueberries, fresh or frozen
- 1 apple, cored, peeled and chipped
- 1 teaspoon freshly grated ginger
- 1 cup filtered water

Directions:
1. Combine all the ingredients in the blender and pulse it on high for 1 minute or until smooth.

Nutrition Info: (Per Serving): Calories-88, Fat- 0 g, Protein- 2 g, Carbohydrates- 20 g

Mint And Avocado Smoothie

Servings: 3
Cooking Time: 5 Minutes
Ingredients:
- 2 cups unsweetened almond milk
- 1 medium banana, chopped
- 2 cups of fresh spinach
- 1 kiwi, peeled and quartered
- Freshly squeezed juice of 1 lime
- 6-8 fresh mint leaves
- ½ avocado, pitted and chopped
- 1 teaspoon freshly grated ginger

Directions:
1. Place all the above listed ingredients in the same order into your blender jar and process it until thick and smooth.

Nutrition Info: (Per Serving): Calories- 254, Fat- 12 g, Protein-10 g, Carbohydrates- 31 g

Ginger Banana Kick

Servings: 2
Cooking Time: 5 Minutes
Ingredients:
- 1 large banana, chopped (fresh or frozen)
- 1 large orange, peeled and de seeded
- 2 cups almond milk or plain soy milk
- 1 teaspoon freshly grated ginger
- ¼ teaspoon vanilla extract
- ½ teaspoon raw, organic honey (optional)
- 1 few ice cubes

Directions:
1. Load your blender jar with the ingredients listed above and puree it until nice and thick.

Nutrition Info: (Per Serving): Calories- 181, Fat- 5.1 g, Proteins- 8.3 g, Carbohydrates- 30 g

Banana-beet Smoothie

Servings: 2
Cooking Time: 5 Minutes
Ingredients:
- 1 cup whole strawberries (fresh or frozen)
- 1 large red beet, peeled and chipped
- 1 large banana (fresh or frozen)
- 1 orange, peeled and de seeded
- 2 cups fresh spinach
- 1 cup fresh kale, stems removed
- 1 cup unsweetened almond milk

Directions:
1. Add everything to the blender jar, secure the lid and pulse until thick and creamy.

Nutrition Info: (Per Serving): Calories- 333, Fat- 4 g, Protein- 10 g, Carbohydrates- 71 g

Pineapple-pear And Spinach Smoothie

Servings: 2
Cooking Time: 5 Minutes
Ingredients:
- 1 cup pineapple, peeled and chopped
- ½ green pear, cored and chopped
- ¾ cup unsweetened almond milk
- 2 cups baby spinach
- 1 cup fresh kale
- 2 tablespoons Chia seeds, soaked
- ¼ teaspoon freshly grated ginger
- 1 teaspoon freshly squeezed lemon juice

Directions:
1. First add the fruits to your blender and whizz for 30 seconds until pureed.
2. Then add the rest f the ingredients and pulse for 1 minute or until a creamy smoothie is got.
3. Pour into tall glasses and enjoy!

Nutrition Info: (Per Serving): Caloris-340, Fat- 0 g, Protein- 8 g, Carbohydrates- 47 g

Hemp-avocado Smoothie

Servings: 2
Cooking Time: 5 Minutes
Ingredients:
- A red apple, cored and chopped
- 1 tablespoon avocado flesh
- 1 cup unsweetened almond milk
- 2 tablespoon hemp seeds
- 2 cups fresh baby spinach

Directions:
1. Pour all the ingredients into your blender and run in on high for 1 minute. Pour into tall glasses and enjoy!
Nutrition Info: (Per Serving): Calories- 350, Fat- 0 g, Protein- 10 g, Carbohydrates- 43 g

Lime And Melon Healer

Servings: 1 Large
Cooking Time: 2 Minutes
Ingredients:
- 1 cup cantaloupe, peeled, deseeded and chopped
- 1 cup honeydew melon, peeled, deseeded and chopped
- Freshly squeezed juice of 1 lime
- 2 teaspoons of raw organic honey
- A pinch of cayenne pepper
- 2-3 cubes of ice (optional)

Directions:
1. Whizz up all the ingredients in your blender, pour into a glass and enjoy!
Nutrition Info: (Per Serving): Calories- 98, Fat- 0 g, Protein-0 g, Carbohydrates- 14 g

Almond- Melon Punch

Servings: 2
Cooking Time: 2 Minutes
Ingredients:
- 2 cups watermelon, deseeded and chopped
- 2 teaspoon almonds, soaked and chopped
- ½ cup plain yogurt
- ½ teaspoon freshly grated ginger
- 1 teaspoon raw organic honey or liquid Stevia
- 3-4 ice cubes

Directions:
1. Add all the ingredients into the blender and pulse until well combined.
Nutrition Info: (Per Serving): Calories- 197, Fat- 2 g, Protein- 7 g, Carbohydrates- 45 g

OVERALL HEALTH AND WELLNESS SMOOTHIES

Cherry- Date Plum Smoothie

Servings: 2
Cooking Time: 5 Minutes
Ingredients:
- ½ cup cherries, pitted
- 1 zucchini, deseeded and chopped
- 1 plum, pitted and chopped
- 1 teaspoon flax seed powder
- 1-2 dates, pitted
- 1 cup filtered water
- 1 teaspoon freshly squeezed lemon juice
- 3-4 ice

Directions:
1. Whizz all the ingredients in the blender until smooth and serve.

Nutrition Info: (Per Serving): Calories- 100, Fat- 0.5 g, Protein- 1.8 g, Carbohydrates- 25 g

Lychee Green Smoothie

Servings: 2
Cooking Time: 2 Minutes
Ingredients:
- 1/3 cup baby spinach
- ½ cup cantaloupe, peeled and chopped
- ½ cup grapes, deseeded
- 3-4 lychees, peeled and pitted
- 1 cup filtered water
- 1 teaspoon freshly squeezed lemon juice
- ½ teaspoon freshly grated ginger
- 3-4 ice cubes

Directions:
1. Just place all the ingredients into the blender and pulse until smooth. Serve immediately!

Nutrition Info: (Per Serving): Calories- 77, Fat- 0.7 g, Protein- 1.9 g, Carbohydrates- 20 g

Crunchy Mango Squash Smoothie

Servings: 2
Cooking Time: 2 Minutes
Ingredients:
- ½ cup squash, peeled and chopped
- ½ cup mango, peeled and chopped
- 1 large orange, peeled and deseeded
- 1 cup filtered water
- 2 teaspoons chopped walnuts
- ½ teaspoon cinnamon powder

- 5-6 ice cubes

Directions:

1. Add all the above ingredients into your blender jar and pulse until thick and frothy.

Nutrition Info: (Per Serving): Calories- 150, Fat- 7.2 g, Protein- 4.2 g, Carbohydrates- 23 g

Apple Cucumber

Servings: 2-3
Cooking Time: 5 Minutes

Ingredients:

- 1 green apple, cored and chopped
- 1 green cucumber, deseeded and chopped
- 1/3 cup collard greens, chopped
- 1 ½ teaspoons Chia seeds, soaked
- 1 tablespoon freshly squeezed lemon juice
- 5-6 fresh mint leaves
- 1 cup filtered water
- 3-4 ice cubes

Directions:

1. Add all the above ingredients into your blender jar and pulse until thick and frothy.

Nutrition Info: (Per Serving): Calories- 114, Fat- 3.2 g, Protein- 3.1 g, Carbohydrates- 25 g

Finana Smoothie

Servings: 2
Cooking Time: 5 Minutes

Ingredients:

- 1 banana, chopped (fresh or frozen)
- 2 figs, chopped
- A handful of mixed greens, washed
- ½ cup filtered water
- 1 teaspoon raw organic honey
- 2-3 ice cubes

Directions:

1. Load your blender with all the ingredients and puree until smoothie is thick and creamy.

Nutrition Info: (Per Serving): Calories- 330, Fat- 1.7 g, Protein- 5.5 g, Carbohydrates- 87 g

Blueberry Cherry Wellness Potion

Servings: 2
Cooking Time: 5 Minutes

Ingredients:

- ¼ cup plain fat free yogurt
- 1/2 cup whole blueberries (fresh or frozen)
- ½ cups cherries, pitted
- A handful of strawberries (fresh or frozen)
- 1 tablespoon fresh avocado flesh
- 1 tablespoon wheatgrass powder
- 1 tablespoon flax seed powder

- 1 tablespoon freshly squeezed lemon juice
- 3-4 ice cubes

Directions:
1. To you blender, add all the above ingredient and pulse until smooth.

Nutrition Info: (Per Serving): Calories- 155, Fat- 5.5 g, Protein- 6.2 g, Carbohydrates- 24 g

Peachyfig Green Smoothie

Servings: 1 Large
Cooking Time: 2 Minutes

Ingredients:
- 1 peach, pitted
- 2 large figs, chopped
- A handful of mixed greens
- ½ cup filtered water
- 2 teaspoon freshly squeezed lemon juice
- 3-4 ice cubes

Directions:
1. Place all the ingredients into the blender, secure the lid and whizz on medium high for 30 seconds or until done. Serve immediately.

Nutrition Info: (Per Serving): Calories-195, Fat- 1.3 g, Protein- 4.5 g, Carbohydrates- 50 g

Mp3 Smoothie

Servings: 2
Cooking Time: 2 Minutes

Ingredients:
- 1 cup papaya, peeled, deseeded and chopped
- 1 large pear, cored and chopped
- 1 cup peaches (fresh or frozen)
- ½ cup plain low fat yogurt
- 1 ½ teaspoon flax seed powder
- 1 teaspoon freshly grated ginger
- 5-6 fresh mint leaves
- 4-5 ice cubes

Directions:
1. To you blender, add all the above ingredient and pulse until smooth.

Nutrition Info: (Per Serving): Calories- 111, Fat- 2.3 g, Protein- 4.7 g, Carbohydrates- 20 g

Trimelon Melba

Servings: 3
Cooking Time: 5 Minutes

Ingredients:
- 1 ¼ cups watermelon, chopped (seedless)
- ½ cup honeydew melon, chopped
- 1 ¼ cup cantaloupe, chopped
- 1 teaspoon raw organic honey
- 2-3 mint leaves

- ¼ cup freshly squeezed orange juice
- 3-4 ice cubes

Directions:
1. Dump all the ingredients into the blender and whip it up until the smoothie is thick and creamy.

Nutrition Info: (Per Serving): Calories-100, Fat- 0.6 g, Protein- 1.9 g, Carbohydrates- 25 g

Apple Blackberry Wonder

Servings: 2
Cooking Time: 2 Minutes
Ingredients:
- 1 cup blackberries (fresh or frozen)
- ½ cup fat free plain yogurt
- 1 tablespoon raw organic honey
- ½ cup freshly prepared apple juice
- ½ banana, sliced
- 2 teaspoon freshly squeezed lemon juice
- 3-4 ice cubes

Directions:
1. Add all the above listed items into the blender and blend until well combined.

Nutrition Info: (Per Serving): Calories- 260, Fat- 0.9 g, Protein- 5.5 g, Carbohydrates- 64 g

Orange Cranberry Smoothie

Servings: 2
Cooking Time: 5 Minutes
Ingredients:
- 1 cup cranberries (fresh or frozen)
- 2/3 cup plain low fat yogurt
- ½ teaspoon vanilla extract
- ½ cup freshly prepared orange juice
- 1 tablespoon raw organic honey
- 1 tablespoon wheat germ
- 5-6 ice cubes

Directions:
1. Place all the above ingredients into the blender jar and process until the mixture is thick and creamy.

Nutrition Info: (Per Serving): Calories- 255, Fat- 1.4 g, Protein- 7.2 g, Carbohydrates- 55 g

Mango Cantaloupe Smoothie

Servings: 2
Cooking Time: 2 Minutes
Ingredients:
- ½ cup mango, peeled and chopped
- ½ cup cantaloupe, peeled and chopped
- ¼ cup pineapple, peeled and chopped
- ¼ cup unsweetened almond milk

- 2 tablespoons almond flakes
- 1 tablespoon freshly squeezed lemon juice
- 3-4 ice cubes

Directions:
1. Dump all the ingredients into the blender and whip it up until the smoothie is thick and creamy.

Nutrition Info: (Per Serving): Calories- 152, Fat- 6.9 g, Protein- 4.3 g, Carbohydrates- 23 g

Avocado- Citrus Blast

Servings: 2-3
Cooking Time: 5 Minutes
Ingredients:
- 1 small tangerine, peeled and deseeded
- ½ cup plain low fat yogurt
- ¼ cup mixed berries
- 1 tablespoon avocado flesh
- 1 tablespoon freshly squeezed lemon juice
- 2 tablespoon freshly squeezed lime juice
- 1 teaspoon flax seed powder
- 2-3 drops vanilla extract
- ½ teaspoon raw organic honey
- 3-4 ice cubes

Directions:
1. Place all the above ingredients into the blender jar and process until the mixture is thick and creamy.

Nutrition Info: (Per Serving): Calories- 245, Fat- 11 g, Protein- 11 g, Carbohydrates- 33 g

Red Healing Potion

Servings: 3
Cooking Time: 5 Minutes
Ingredients:
- 2 cups fresh coconut water
- 1 ½ cup pomegranate seeds
- 1 ¼ cup of red grapes, deseeded
- 1 cup whole strawberries (fresh or frozen)
- 2 tablespoons freshly squeezed lemon juice
- 4-5 ice cubes

Directions:
1. Place everything in your blender jar and whizz until smooth and frothy.

Nutrition Info: (Per Serving): Calories- 182, Fat-1.2 g, Protein- 4.3 g, Carbohydrates- 44 g

LOW FAT SMOOTHIES

Super Veggie Smoothie

Servings: 3- 4
Cooking Time: 5 Minutes
Ingredients:
- 1 large carrot, peeled and chopped
- ½ cup broccoli florets
- 1 large apple, cored and chopped
- 2 handfuls of baby spinach, washed and chopped
- 2 large oranges, peeled and seeded
- 1 tablespoons freshly squeezed lemon juice
- ½ cup filtered water

Directions:
1. Load your blender jar with the above listed items and process until smooth.

Nutrition Info: (Per Serving): Calories- 326, Fat- 1.1 g, Protein- 7.5 g, Carbohydrates- 80 g

Simple Cherry Berry Wonder

Servings: 3
Cooking Time: 5 Minutes
Ingredients:
- ¾ cup whole strawberries (fresh or frozen)
- A handful of blueberries (fresh or frozen)
- ½ cup raspberries (fresh or frozen)
- ½ cup pitted berries (fresh or frozen)
- ½ cup freshly prepared pomegranate juice
- 2 teaspoons freshly squeezed lemon juice
- 3-4 ice cubes

Directions:
1. Add all the ingredients in the same order as listed above and blend until smooth and thick

Nutrition Info: (Per Serving): Calories-105, Fat- 0.2 g, Protein- 19 g, Carbohydrates- 27 g

Cantaloupe Berry Blast

Servings: 2
Cooking Time: 2 Minutes
Ingredients:
- 1 cup cantaloupe, chopped
- 1 cup whole blueberries (fresh or frozen)
- ½ cup unsweetened almond milk
- 1 tablespoon Chia seeds
- 1 teaspoon, raw organic honey
- 2-3 ice cubes

Directions:
1. Load your high speed blender jar with all the ingredients and puree until thick and smooth.

Nutrition Info: (Per Serving): Calories- 120, Fat- 3.3 g, Protein- 3.5 g, Carbohydrates- 37 g

Low Fat Tropical Pleasure

Servings: 4
Cooking Time: 5 Minutes
Ingredients:
- 1 cup banana, chopped (fresh or frozen)
- 1 cup mango, chopped (fresh or frozen)
- 1 cup kiwi, peeled and chopped (fresh or frozen)
- 1 cup pineapple, chopped (fresh or frozen)
- ½ cup freshly squeezed orange juice
- 1 cup low fat buttermilk
- 4-5 ice cubes

Directions:
1. Place all the ingredients into the high speed blender jar and run it on high for 20 seconds until everything is well combined. Pour into serving glass and enjoy!

Nutrition Info: (Per Serving): Calories-220, Fat- 14 g, Protein- 4 g, Carbohydrates- 48 g

Banana Orange Pina Colada

Servings: 4
Cooking Time: 5 Minutes
Ingredients:
- 1 ripe banana, chopped (fresh or frozen)
- 1 cup freshly prepared pineapple juice
- 1 cup plain low fat yogurt
- ¼ teaspoon vanilla extract
- 1 cup freshly prepared orange juice
- 2 teaspoons freshly squeezed lemon juice
- 3-4 ice cubes

Directions:
1. Combine all the ingredients in a blender jar and run it for 1 minute or until smooth and creamy.

Nutrition Info: (Per Serving): Calories- 145, Fat- 0 g, Protein- 3 g, Carbohydrates- 33 g

Pomegranate- Ginger Melba

Servings: 3
Cooking Time: 2 Minutes
Ingredients:
- 2 cups freshly prepared pomegranate juice
- 2 bananas, chopped (fresh or frozen)
- 1 cup low fat plain Greek yogurt
- 1 teaspoon freshly grated ginger
- 5-6 ice cubes

Directions:

1. Place all the ingredients into your blender and run it on medium high speed for 1-2 minutes or until done.
Nutrition Info: (Per Serving): Calories- 195, Fat- 2.2 g, Protein- 8 g, Carbohydrates- 40 g

The Summer Hearty Shake

Servings: 2
Cooking Time: 5 Minutes
Ingredients:
- 1 cup frozen blackberries
- ¾ cup whole milk vanilla yogurt
- ½ cup unsweetened vanilla almond milk
- ½ cup frozen strawberries
- ½ cup frozen peaches
- 1 tablespoon hemp seeds
- Dash of ground cinnamon

Directions:
1. Add all the ingredients except vegetables/fruits first
2. Blend until smooth
3. Add the vegetable/fruits
4. Blend until smooth
5. Add a few ice cubes and serve the smoothie
6. Enjoy!

Nutrition Info: Calories: 187; Fat: 6g; Carbohydrates: 23g; Protein: 6g

Green Tea Berry Classic Smoothie

Servings: 1
Cooking Time: 5 Minutes
Ingredients:
- ¼ cups concentrated green tea (1 tea bag+ ¼ cup water)
- ½ cup plain low fat yogurt
- ¼ teaspoon vanilla extract
- 1 ½ teaspoon raw organic honey
- ¼ cup mixed berries
- Pinch of cinnamon powder
- Pinch of nutmeg powder
- 3-4 ice cubes

Directions:
1. Combine all the ingredients in a blender jar and run it for 1 minute or until smooth and creamy.
Nutrition Info: (Per Serving): Calories- 265, Fat- 4.5 g, Protein- 10 g, Carbohydrates- 50 g

The Great Shamrock Shake

Servings: 1
Cooking Time: 10 Minutes

Ingredients:
- 1 cup coconut milk, unsweetened
- 1 avocado, peeled, pitted and sliced
- 1 tablespoon pure vanilla extract
- 1 teaspoon pure peppermint extract
- Liquid stevia
- 1 cup ice

Directions:
1. Add all the listed ingredients into your blender
2. Blend until smooth
3. Serve chilled and enjoy!

Nutrition Info: Calories: 195; Fat: 19g; Carbohydrates: 4.4g; Protein: 2g

Sage Blackberry

Servings: 2
Cooking Time: 5 Minutes
Ingredients:
- 1-ounce blackberries
- 3 tablespoons cashew
- 1 pear, chopped
- 4 ounces pineapple
- 3 sage leaves
- ½ teaspoon maqui berry powder

Directions:
1. Add all the listed ingredients to a blender
2. Blend until you have a smooth and creamy texture
3. Serve chilled and enjoy!

Nutrition Info: Calories: 154; Fat: 6g; Carbohydrates: 24g; Protein: 3g

Mini Pepper Popper Smoothie

Servings: 2
Cooking Time: 5 Minutes
Ingredients:
- 5 ounces mini peppers, seeded
- 4 ounces pineapple
- 1 orange, peeled
- 3 tablespoons almonds
- ½ lemon, juiced
- 1 cup of water
- 1 teaspoon rose hip powder

Directions:
1. Add all the listed ingredients to a blender
2. Blend until you have a smooth and creamy texture
3. Serve chilled and enjoy!

Nutrition Info: Calories: 190; Fat: 8g; Carbohydrates: 21g; Protein: 5g

Mango Passion Smoothie

Servings: 4
Cooking Time: 5 Minutes
Ingredients:
- 2 cups mango, chopped (fresh or frozen)
- 1 ½ cups plain nonfat yogurt
- ¼ teaspoon vanilla extract
- 1 cup freshly prepared passion fruit juice
- ½ cup filtered water
- 2 tablespoon freshly squeezed lemon juice
- 4-5 ice cubes

Directions:
1. To you blender, add the above ingredient and pulse until smooth.

Nutrition Info: (Per Serving): Calories- 290, Fat-2 g, Protein- 10 g, Carbohydrates- 61 g

ANTI-AGEING SMOOTHIES

Raspberry Goji Berry Duet

Servings: 3-4
Cooking Time: 5 Minutes
Ingredients:
- 2 cups fresh coconut water
- 1/3 cup Goji berries
- 1 cup raspberries (fresh or frozen)
- 1 avocado, peeled, pitted and chopped
- 1 large banana, sliced (fresh or frozen)
- 1 tablespoon Chia sees, soaked
- 1 tablespoon flaxseed
- 1 tablespoon raw organic honey
- 1 teaspoon freshly squeezed lemon juice
- 3-4 ice cubes

Directions:
1. Load the blender with all the ingredients listed above and pulse it on medium for 45 seconds or until done.

Nutrition Info: (Per Serving): Calories- 412, Fat- 15 g, Protein- 10 g, Carbohydrates- 65 g

Hazelnut And Banana Crunch

Servings: 1 Large
Cooking Time: 2 Minutes
Ingredients:
- ¾ cup unsweetened almond milk
- 1 large banana, sliced (fresh or frozen)
- ¼ cup hazelnuts, chopped
- ¼ teaspoon nutmeg powder
- 1 teaspoon raw, organic honey
- 1-2 ice cubes

Directions:
1. Add everything to the blender and pulse until smooth. Serve chilled!

Nutrition Info: (Per Serving): Calories- 221, Fat- 9.5 g, Protein- 7.8 g, Carbohydrates- 25 g

Coconut Mulberry Banana Smoothie

Servings: 3
Cooking Time: 5 Minutes
Ingredients:
- 1 cup mulberries (fresh or frozen)
- 2 cups fresh coconut water
- 1/3 cup cranberries
- 1 large banana, chopped (fresh or frozen)
- 1 apple, cored and chopped
- 1 tablespoon hemp seeds

- 1 tablespoon flax seeds
- Freshly squeezed juice of ½ lime
- ½ cup ice cubes

Directions:

1. To your high speed blender, add all the items listed above and blitz until everything is well combined.

Nutrition Info: (Per Serving): Calories- 322, Fat- 15 g, Protein- 10 g, Carbohydrates- 70 g

Maca – Mango Delight

Servings: 2
Cooking Time: 5 Minutes
Ingredients:
- 1 cup fresh coconut water
- 1 cup freshly prepared carrot juice or 1 ½ cup chopped carrot
- 1 large mango, peeled and chopped
- ½ teaspoon maca root powder
- ½ teaspoon cinnamon powder
- 1 teaspoon freshly squeezed lemon juice
- 3-4 ice cubes

Directions:

1. Into the blender jar, add all of the ingredients mentioned above and whizz until smooth.

Nutrition Info: (Per Serving): Calories- 220, Fat-0 g, Protein- 3 g, Carbohydrates- 10 g

Super Duper Berry Smoothie

Servings: 2
Cooking Time: 5 Minutes
Ingredients:
- ½ cup unsweetened almond milk
- ½ cup frozen blueberries
- ½ cup whole strawberries (fresh or frozen)
- ¼ cup blackberries (fresh or frozen)
- ½ cup red cherries, pitted (fresh or frozen)
- 1 tablespoon cacao powder
- ½ cup romaine lettuce
- 1 teaspoon Chia seeds, soaked
- 1 teaspoon Spirulina powder
- 1 tablespoon hemp powder
- 2-3 ice cubes

Directions:

1. To make this smoothie, add all the ingredients into the blender and blitz for 45 seconds on medium high speed.
2. Pour into servings glasses and enjoy!

Nutrition Info: (Per Serving): Calories- 345, Fat- 20 g, Protein- 18 g, Carbohydrates- 75 g

Powerful Kale And Carrot Glass

Servings: 1
Cooking Time: 10 Minutes
Ingredients:
- 1 cup of coconut water
- Lemon juice, 1 lemon
- 1 green apple, core removed and chopped
- 1 carrot, chopped
- 1 cup kale

Directions:
1. Add all the listed ingredients to a blender
2. Blend until you have a smooth and creamy texture
3. Serve chilled and enjoy!

Nutrition Info: Calories: 116; Fat: 5g; Carbohydrates: 14g; Protein: 6g

Watermelon- Yogurt Smoothie

Servings: 2
Cooking Time: 5 Minutes
Ingredients:
- 2 cups watermelon chopped (fresh or frozen)
- ½ cup plain yogurt
- 1 tablespoon almond butter
- 1 teaspoon raw organic honey
- ½ teaspoon freshly grated ginger
- 4-5 ice cubes

Directions:
1. Add all the ingredients into the blender and pulse until smooth.

Nutrition Info: (Per Serving): Calories- 112, Fat- 1.7 g, Protein-4.4 g, Carbohydrates- 22.4 g

Spiced Blackberry Smoothie

Servings: 2-3
Cooking Time: 5 Minutes
Ingredients:
- 1 cup fresh coconut water
- 1 cup whole blackberries (fresh or frozen)
- 1 cup beetroot (peeled and boiled)
- 1 pear, cored and chopped
- ½ cup kale , stems removed and chopped
- 1 tablespoon hemp seed powder
- ¼ teaspoon cinnamon powder
- ¼ teaspoon nutmeg powder
- ½ teaspoon freshly grated ginger
- 1 teaspoon freshly squeezed lemon juice
- 4-5 ice cubes (optional)

Directions:
1.   Place all the above listed items into the blender and run it on high for 30 seconds until everything is well blended.
Nutrition Info: (Per Serving): Calories- 240, Fat-6 g, Protein- 5.1 g, Carbohydrates- 38 g

Beets And Berry Beauty Enhancer

Servings: 2
Cooking Time: 5 Minutes
Ingredients:
- 1 teaspoon ginger, grated
- 2 tablespoons pumpkin seeds
- ¼ cup avocado, chopped
- ¼ cup beet, steamed and peeled
- 1/3 cup frozen strawberries
- 1/3 cup frozen raspberries
- 1/3 cup frozen blueberries
- ½ cup Greek yogurt
- ½ cup unsweetened almond milk

Directions:
1.   Add all the ingredients except vegetables/fruits first
2.   Blend until smooth
3.   Add the vegetable/fruits
4.   Blend until smooth
5.   Add a few ice cubes and serve the smoothie
6.   Enjoy!
Nutrition Info: Calories: 418; Fat: 20g; Carbohydrates: 50g; Protein: 17g

A Tropical Glass Of Chia

Servings: 1
Cooking Time: 10 Minutes
Ingredients:
- 1 cup coconut water
- 1 tablespoon chia seeds
- 1 cup pineapple, sliced
- ½ cup mango, sliced

Directions:
1.   Add all the listed ingredients to a blender
2.   Blend until you have a smooth and creamy texture
3.   Serve chilled and enjoy!
Nutrition Info: Calories: 90; Fat: 5g; Carbohydrates: 11g; Protein: 4g

A Green Grape Shake

Servings: 2
Cooking Time: 5 Minutes

Ingredients:
- 1 cup ice
- 2 tablespoons chia seeds
- 1 orange, peeled and quartered
- 1 pear, cored and chopped
- 1 cup green seedless grapes
- 2 cups baby kale
- ½ frozen banana, sliced
- ½ cup silken tofu
- ½ cup of water

Directions:
1. Add all the ingredients except vegetables/fruits first
2. Blend until smooth
3. Add the vegetable/fruits
4. Blend until smooth
5. Add a few ice cubes and serve the smoothie
6. Enjoy!

Nutrition Info: Calories: 86; Fat: 8g; Carbohydrates: 3g; Protein: 2g

DIGESTION SUPPORT SMOOTHIES

Hemp-melon Refresher

Servings: 1-2
Cooking Time: 2 Minutes
Ingredients:
- 1 ½ cup melon, chopped
- 1 large banana, chopped
- 1 teaspoon freshly grated ginger
- 2 teaspoons hemp seed powder
- ¾ cup filtered water
- 2-4 cubes of ice
- 1 inch of cinnamon powder

Directions:
1. Place all the items listed above into the blender jar and process until the smoothie is thick and creamy.

Nutrition Info: (Per Serving): Calories- 120, Fat- 2 g, Protein- 3.1 g, Carbohydrates- 27 g

Blueberry Chia Smoothie

Servings: 2
Cooking Time: 10 Minutes
Ingredients:
- 2 cups blueberries, frozen
- 1 cup coconut cream
- 4 tablespoons coconut oil
- 4 tablespoons swerve sweetener
- 4 tablespoons chia seeds, ground
- 2 cups full-fat Greek yogurt
- 2 cups almond milk, unsweetened

Directions:
1. Add all the listed ingredients to a blender
2. Blend until you have a smooth and creamy texture
3. Serve chilled and enjoy!

Nutrition Info: Calories: 351; Fat: 36g; Carbohydrates: 12.8g; Protein: 12.9g

Tropical Storm Glass

Servings: 2
Cooking Time: 5 Minutes
Ingredients:
- 1 tablespoon hemp seeds
- ¾ cup plain coconut yogurt
- 1 fresh banana
- 1 cup unsweetened coconut milk
- 1½ cups frozen papaya blend (mix of papaya, mango, strawberry, and pineapple)

Directions:

1. Add all the ingredients except vegetables/fruits first
2. Blend until smooth
3. Add the vegetable/fruits
4. Blend until smooth
5. Add a few ice cubes and serve the smoothie
6. Enjoy!

Nutrition Info: Calories: 186; Fat: 0g; Carbohydrates: 14g; Protein: 1g

Grape And Nectarine Blende

Servings: 1
Cooking Time: 5 Minutes
Ingredients:

- 1 cup red or green grapes, seedless
- 1 large nectarine, peeled and chopped
- 1 cup plain yogurt
- 1 teaspoon freshly squeezed lemon juice
- 1 teaspoon raw organic honey
- ¼ teaspoon cinnamon powder
- 1/3 cup filtered water

Directions:
1. To your high speed blender jar, add the ingredients and puree it until creamy and thick.

Nutrition Info: (Per Serving): Calories- 201, Fat- 2.2 g, Protein- 8.9 g, Carbohydrates- 32 g

Papaya- Mint Chiller

Servings: 2
Cooking Time: 2 Minutes
Ingredients:

- 1 ½ cups papaya, chopped (frozen)
- ½ cup plain yogurt
- 1 tablespoon regularly grated ginger
- 1 tablespoon of freshly squeezed lemon juice
- 1 teaspoon raw, organic honey or liquid Stevia
- 5-7 mint leaves
- A handful of ice cubes

Directions:
1. To your blender jar, add the ingredients one by one and process till you get a thick, creamy consistency.

Nutrition Info: (Per Serving): Calories- 177, Fat- 1.2 g, Protein-8.2 g, Carbohydrates- 41 g

Almond And Date Smoothie

Servings: 2
Cooking Time: 5 Minutes
Ingredients:

- 1 cup unsweetened almond milk

- 3 teaspoons almond butter
- 2 cups baby spinach, washed and chopped
- 1 large apple, cored and chopped
- 1/3 teaspoon vanilla extract
- 2-3 medjool dates, pitted
- A pinch of cinnamon powder
- A pinch of Celtic salt
- 2-3 ice cubes

Directions:
1. Combine all the above listed items in the blender jar and whip it up nice and smooth. Pour into 2 servings lasses and enjoy.

Nutrition Info: (Per Serving): Calories- 500, Fat- 19 g, Protein- 11 g, Carbohydrates- 82 g

Chia-berry Belly Blaster

Servings: 2
Cooking Time: 5 Minutes
Ingredients:
- 1 cup berries, frozen
- 1 cup plain Greek yogurt, unsweetened
- 1 tablespoon chia seeds, ground
- 1 tablespoon vanilla extract
- ½ cup ice

Directions:
1. Add all the listed ingredients to a blender
2. Blend until you have a smooth and creamy texture
3. Serve chilled and enjoy!

Nutrition Info: Calories: 148; Fat: 5g; Carbohydrates: 26g; Protein: 4g

A Minty Drink

Servings: 2
Cooking Time: 5 Minutes
Ingredients:
- 1 tablespoon hemp seeds
- Fresh mint leaves
- ¾ cup plain coconut yogurt
- 1 cup frozen mango
- 1 cup frozen strawberries
- 1 cup unsweetened vanilla almond milk

Directions:
1. Add all the ingredients except vegetables/fruits first
2. Blend until smooth
3. Add the vegetable/fruits
4. Blend until smooth
5. Add a few ice cubes and serve the smoothie
6. Enjoy!

Nutrition Info: Calories: 391; Fat: 10g; Carbohydrates: 44g; Protein: 5g

The Baked Apple

Servings: 2
Cooking Time: 5 Minutes
Ingredients:
- Dash ground cinnamon
- 1 tablespoon rolled oats
- 1 tablespoon hemp seeds
- ¾ cup Siggi's Whole milk vanilla yogurt
- 1 cup pear chunks
- 1 cup apple chunks
- 1 cup unsweetened vanilla almond milk

Directions:
1. Add all the ingredients except vegetables/fruits first
2. Blend until smooth
3. Add the vegetable/fruits
4. Blend until smooth
5. Add a few ice cubes and serve the smoothie
6. Enjoy!

Nutrition Info: Calories: 160; Fat: 4g; Carbohydrates: 33g; Protein: 2g

Sapodilla, Chia And Almond Milk Smoothie

Servings: 2
Cooking Time: 5 Minutes
Ingredients:
- 4 medium sapodillas
- 2/3 cup almond milk
- 3 tablespoons chia seeds
- 1 tablespoon flakes

Directions:
1. Wash the sapodillas, peel them and then roughly chop them
2. Toss the chopped sapodillas into your blender
3. Then add almond milk
4. Add all the listed ingredients to a blender
5. Blend well and add almond on top
6. Serve and enjoy!

Nutrition Info: Calories: 113; Fat: 1g; Carbohydrates: 21g; Protein: 5g

ANTI-INFLAMMATORY SMOOTHIES

Tangy Ginger & Radish Smoothie

Servings: 2
Cooking Time: 10 Minutes
Ingredients:
- 1 orange, peeled, seeded and sliced
- 1 radish, trimmed and chopped
- 1 tablespoon fresh ginger, peeled and chopped
- 5-10 fresh mint leaves
- 1 tablespoon ground chia seeds
- 1 teaspoon organic honey
- 1 cup spring water
- ½ cup fresh orange juice
- 1 tablespoon fresh lemon juice
- Ice, as required

Directions:
1. In a high speed blender, add all ingredients and pulse till smooth.
2. Transfer into 2 glasses and serve immediately.

Berries, Watermelon & Avocado Smoothie

Servings: 1
Cooking Time: 10 Minutes
Ingredients:
- 1½ cups mixed frozen berries
- 1 cup watermelon, peeled, seeded and chopped
- ¼ avocado, peeled, pitted and chopped
- 1 inch fresh ginger piece, peeled and chopped
- 2 teaspoons chia seeds
- ¾ cup fresh coconut water

Directions:
1. In a high speed blender, add all ingredients and pulse till smooth.
2. Transfer into a glass and serve immediately.

Kiwi Kiss Smoothie

Servings: 1
Cooking Time: 5 Minutes
Ingredients:
- 2 kiwifruits, peeled and chopped
- 1 cup mango, chopped
- 1 orange, peeled and chopped
- ¾ cup of filtered water (to adjust consistency)

Directions:
1. Add all the 3 chopped fruits and water into the blender and blend it for 45 seconds or until a lump free, mixture is got.

2. Pour into a serving glass and enjoy this delicious smoothie.
Nutrition Info: (Per Serving): Calories-354, Fats-2 g, Protein- 8 g, Carbohydrates-87 g

Chia And Cherry Smoothie

Servings: 1
Cooking Time: 5 Minutes
Ingredients:
- A handful of fresh cherries
- ½ cup of pineapple, cubed
- A couple of beetroot pieces
- 1 tablespoon of Chia seeds
- 2-3 ice cubes (optional)
- 8 ounces of coconut water
- 1 teaspoon of coconut oil

Directions:
1. Wash the cherries, pineapple and beetroot before chipping them and place in a blender.
2. Add the remaining ingredients to the jar and run it on high for 1 minute until smooth.
3. Serve chilled.
Nutrition Info: (Per Serving): Calories- 250, Fat-4.5 g, Protein- 6 g, Carbohydrates-51 g

Mango-pina Smoothie

Servings: 1
Cooking Time: 2 Minutes
Ingredients:
- 1 mango, chopped
- 1 cup of pineapple, cubed
- 1handful of baby spinach
- 1 cup of filtered water

Directions:
1. Wash the pineapple and mango thoroughly before peeling and chopping into cubes.
2. Next, add all the ingredients into the blender and whir it up for 45 seconds to 1 minute until thick and frothy.
Nutrition Info: (Per Serving): Calories-219, Fat-0.8 g, protein- 3.9 g, carbohydrates -57.8 g

Cherry & Kale Smoothie

Servings: 1
Cooking Time: 10 Minutes
Ingredients:
- 2 ripe bananas, peeled and sliced
- 1 cup fresh cherries, pitted
- 1 cup fresh kale, trimmed
- 1 teaspoon fresh ginger, peeled and chopped
- 1 tablespoon chia seeds, soaked for 15 minutes
- ½ teaspoon ground turmeric
- ¼ teaspoon ground cinnamon
- 1 cup coconut water

Directions:
1. In a high speed blender, add all ingredients and pulse till smooth.
2. Transfer into a glass and serve immediately.

Cherry & Blueberry Smoothie

Servings: 1
Cooking Time: 10 Minutes
Ingredients:
- 2 cups escarole
- ½ cup frozen blueberries
- ½ cup frozen cherries
- ¼ teaspoon ground cinnamon
- ¼ teaspoon ground turmeric
- 1 scoop of chocolate protein powder
- 1 cup filtered water
- 5 ice cubes, crushed

Directions:
1. In a high speed blender, add all ingredients and pulse till smooth.
2. Transfer into a glass and serve immediately.

Pineapple & Orange Smoothie

Servings: 1
Cooking Time: 10 Minutes
Ingredients:
- 1 fresh orange, peeled and chopped
- 1½ cups fresh pineapple, chopped
- 1 small thumb of ginger, peeled and chopped/grated
- 1 frozen banana, peeled and sliced
- 1 teaspoon ground turmeric
- 1 tablespoon chia seeds
- 1 cup unsweetened almond milk

Directions:
1. In a high speed blender, add all ingredients and pulse till smooth.
2. Transfer into a glass and serve immediately.

Veggies & Turmeric Smoothie

Servings: 2
Cooking Time: 10 Minutes
Ingredients:
- 1 small avocado, peeled, pitted and chopped
- ½ of green bell pepper, seeded and chopped
- 1-inch fresh turmeric piece, peeled and grated
- 1 cup fresh baby spinach, chopped
- 1 cup fresh arugula, chopped
- 1-inch fresh ginger piece, peeled and chopped
- ¾ cups fresh parsley

- Pinch of cayenne pepper
- Pinch of salt
- 1 cup fresh coconut water

Directions:
1. In a high speed blender, add all ingredients and pulse till smooth.
2. Transfer into 2 glasses and serve immediately.

Pineapple, Avocado & Spinach Smoothie

Servings: 2
Cooking Time: 10 Minutes
Ingredients:
- ¼ of pineapple, peeled and chopped
- 3 cups spinach, chopped
- ¼ of avocado, peeled, pitted and chopped
- ¼ cup fresh cilantro, chopped
- ½-inch fresh ginger piece, peeled and chopped
- 1 tablespoon chia seeds
- 1 tablespoon ground turmeric
- Fresh cracked black pepper, to taste

Directions:
1. In a high speed blender, add all ingredients and pulse till smooth.
2. Transfer into a glass and serve immediately.

Turmeric-mango Smoothie

Servings: 2
Cooking Time: 5 Minutes
Ingredients:
- 2 cups unsweetened almond milk
- 1 banana (fresh or frozen)
- 1 cup papaya, chopped (fresh or frozen)
- 1 cup mango, chopped
- 1 teaspoon freshly grated turmeric
- Pinch of black pepper
- ½ teaspoon finely grated ginger
- 1 tablespoon raw organic honey
- ½ teaspoon vanilla extract

Directions:
1. For this recipe, you need to prepare a turmeric milk concoction before you make the smoothie.
2. Heat a sauce pan on medium high and boil the almond milk, along with the turmeric, black pepper, ginger and honey.
3. Let it simmer for 5 minutes on low.
4. Allow this mixture to cool completely.
5. Once it has cooled, load your blender with this concoction, and all the remaining ingredients and process it until smooth.

Nutrition Info: (Per Serving): Calories-262, Fats-10 g, Proteins- 5.8 g, Carbohydrates-40.6 g

Tangy Mango & Spinach Smoothie

Servings: 2
Cooking Time: 10 Minutes
Ingredients:
- 2 cups frozen mango, peeled, pitted and chopped
- 3 cups fresh spinach, chopped
- 1 teaspoon ground turmeric
- 16-ounce fresh coconut water
- 1 tablespoon lemon juice
- 1 tablespoon lime juice

Directions:
1. In a high speed blender, add all ingredients and pulse till smooth.
2. Transfer into 2 glasses and serve immediately.

Green Goblin Smoothie

Servings: 1
Cooking Time: 5 Minutes
Ingredients:
- 1 ½ cups of seedless green grapes
- ¼ cup freshly squeezed lemon juice
- ¼ cup avocado, chopped
- A handful of flat leaf parsley, washed and chopped
- 1 teaspoons freshly grated ginger
- 2-3 drops of raw organic honey or liquid Stevia
- 2-3 ice cubes

Directions:
1. Add all the ingredients into your blender and pulse for 1 minute and serve.
Nutrition Info: (Per Serving): Calories-244, Fat-6 g, Protein-4g, Carbohydrates-50 g

Banana & Ginger Smoothie

Servings: 1
Cooking Time: 10 Minutes
Ingredients:
- 1-inch fresh ginger piece, peeled and chopped
- 1 frozen banana, peeled and sliced
- ½ teaspoon ground cinnamon
- 1 cup coconut milk

Directions:
1. In a high speed blender, add all ingredients and pulse till smooth.
2. Transfer into a glass and serve immediately.

MUSCLE, BONE AND JOINT SMOOTHIES

Orange Gold Smoothie

Servings: 2
Cooking Time: 5 Minutes
Ingredients:
- ½ cup fresh coconut milk
- ½ cup mango, chopped
- ½ cup pineapple, chopped
- ½ cup peaches, pitted
- ½ teaspoon freshly grated lemon zest
- ¼ teaspoon cinnamon powder
- ¼ teaspoon nutmeg powder
- ½ teaspoon cayenne pepper
- A pinch of Celtic salt
- ¾ cup filtered water
- A handful of ice cubes

Directions:
1. Place all the ingredients into the blender and whizz until thick and smooth.

Nutrition Info: (Per Serving): Calories- 171, Fat- 4.4 g, Protein- 2.9 g, Carbohydrates- 35 g

Strawberry-avocado Smoothie

Servings: 2
Cooking Time: 2 Minutes
Ingredients:
- 1 cup strawberries (fresh or frozen)
- ½ avocado, peeled, pitted and chopped
- 1 small pear, cored and chopped
- 1 small banana, sliced (fresh or frozen)
- 1 cup green lettuce (iceberg or romaine)
- ½ cup dandelion greens
- 1-2 chard leaves
- 1 cup filtered water
- 2-3 ice cubes

Directions:
1. Place all the ingredients in the blender and process until smooth. Serve chilled.

Nutrition Info: (Per Serving): Calories- 345, Fat- 7.9g, Protein- 5 g, Carbohydrates- 70 g

Kiwi Quick Smoothie

Servings: 2
Cooking Time: 2 Minutes
Ingredients:
- ½ cup unsweetened almond milk
- ½ cup plain yoghurt

- ¼ cup fresh coconut milk
- ½ cup whole strawberries (fresh or frozen)
- 1 kiwi, peeled and chopped
- 1 teaspoon raw, organic honey
- ½ teaspoon Chia seeds

Directions:
1. Combine all the ingredients in a high speed blender and process until smooth.

Nutrition Info: (Per Serving): Calories- 260, Fat- 9 g, Protein- 13 g, Carbohydrates- 37 g

Maca –banana Smoothie

Servings: 2-3
Cooking Time: 5 Minutes
Ingredients:
- 1 cup fresh coconut water
- 1 tablespoon almond butter
- 1 ½ medium banana, chopped (fresh or frozen)
- ½ tablespoon maca powder
- ½ cup fresh baby spinach, washed and chopped
- 1 teaspoon Chia seeds
- A pinch of cinnamon powder
- 2-3 ice cubes

Directions:
1. Load the blender with all the ingredients and process on medium speed for 30 second or until smoothie is thick and creamy.

Nutrition Info: (Per Serving): Calories- 430, Fat- 19.8 g, Protein- 12 g, Carbohydrates- 58 g

Berry-cantaloupe Smoothie

Servings: 3
Cooking Time: 5 Minutes
Ingredients:
- ½ cup whole strawberries (fresh or frozen)
- 1 cup mango, chopped
- 1 cups cantaloupe, chopped
- ½ cup fresh kale, stems removed
- 1 celery stalks, chopped
- 1 chard leaves, chopped
- A small handful of parsley
- ¼ cup baby spinach
- ½ cup filtered water

Directions:
1. Pour all the ingredients into a high speed blender and run in on high for 2 seconds or until the desired consistency is got.

Nutrition Info: (Per Serving): Calories- 375, Fat- 1.9 g, Protein- 6.8 g, Carbohydrates- 95 g

Spinach And Kiwi Smoothie

Servings: 2-3
Cooking Time: 2 Minutes
Ingredients:
- 1 cup fresh coconut milk
- 1 ½ cup fresh baby spinach
- ½ cup arugula, chopped
- 1 cup kiwi, peeled and chopped
- 1 small banana, chopped
- 1 teaspoon freshly squeezed lemon juice

Directions:
1. Add all the ingredients to a high speed blender and pulse until smooth. Pour into glasses and serve.

Nutrition Info: (Per Serving): Calories- 130, Fat- 2.1 g, Protein- 2 g, Carbohydrates- 29 g

Cucumber- Pear Healer

Servings: 2
Cooking Time: 2 Minutes
Ingredients:
- 1 cup unsweetened almond milk
- 2 cups cucumber, chopped
- 2 large pears, cored and chopped
- 8-9 fresh mint leaves
- 1 teaspoon freshly squeezed lemon juice
- 1 teaspoon raw organic honey
- 3-4 ice cubes

Directions:
1. Just add all the ingredients into the blender and pulse until smooth.

Nutrition Info: (Per Serving): Calories- 285, Fat- 4.8 g, Protein- 5 g, Carbohydrates- 65 g

Fruit "n" Nut Smoothie

Servings: 2
Cooking Time: 5 Minutes
Ingredients:
- 1 cup freshly brewed green tea
- 1 cup red cherries, pitted
- 1 cup whole strawberries (fresh or frozen)
- ½ kale, stems removed
- ¼ cup walnuts, halved
- ½ teaspoon freshly grated ginger
- 1 teaspoon wheat grass powder
- 1 teaspoon hemp powder

Directions:
1. Load all the ingredients in a high speed blender and process until it is smooth and thick.

Nutrition Info: (Per Serving): Calories- 255, Fat- 11 g, Protein- 8.9 g, Carbohydrates- 38 g

Apple –kiwi Blush

Servings: 2
Cooking Time: 5 Minutes
Ingredients:
- 1 cup unsweetened almond milk
- 1 large apple, cored and chopped
- 2 kiwi fruits, peeled and chopped
- 1 cup cucumber, chopped
- 2-3 collard green leaves, stems removed and chopped
- 3 teaspoons Chia seeds, soaked
- 2-3 ice cubes (optional)

Directions:
1. Place all the ingredients in a high speed bender and blitz on medium speed for 30 seconds or until smooth.

Nutrition Info: (Per Serving): Calories- 340, Fat- 0.5 g, Protein- 11 g, Carbohydrates- 60 g

Coconut-blueberry Smoothie

Servings: 3
Cooking Time: 5 Minutes
Ingredients:
- 1 cup fresh coconut water
- 1 cup blueberries
- 1 large banana, sliced (fresh or frozen)
- 1 cup baby spinach, washed and chopped
- ½ cup fresh kale, stems removed and chopped
- ½ cup dandelion greens chopped
- 1 teaspoon freshly squeezed lemon juice

Directions:
1. Place all the ingredients into the blender and blitz until smooth.

Nutrition Info: (Per Serving): Calories- 250, Fat- 1.1 g, Protein- 4 g, Carbohydrates- 60 g

Pineapple Sage Smoothie

Servings: 2
Cooking Time: 5 Minutes
Ingredients:
- 1 cup pineapple, peeled and chopped
- 1 pear, core and chopped
- 2-3 sage leaves
- 1 teaspoon Chia seeds, soaked
- 1 teaspoon hemp seed powder
- 1 teaspoon freshly squeezed lemon juice

- ¾ cup water
- 2-3 ice cubes

Directions:
1. Add all the ingredients into the blender and run it on high for 30 seconds or until well combined.

Nutrition Info: (Per Serving): Calories- 250, Fat- 1.1 g, Protein- 5 g , Carbohydrates- 87 g

Ginger- Papaya Smoothie

Servings: 2
Cooking Time: 5 Minutes
Ingredients:
- 1 cup plain yogurt
- 1 ¼ cup papaya, chopped
- 1 tablespoon raw organic honey
- ¼ teaspoon freshly grated ginger
- 1 teaspoon freshly squeezed lemon juice
- 4-5 ice cubes

Directions:
1. Add all the ingredients into the blender, secure the lid and pulse into smooth.

Nutrition Info: (Per Serving): Calories- 140, Fat- 3.4 g, Protein- 6.1 g, Carbohydrates- 25 g

Orange Kiwi Punch

Servings: 2-3
Cooking Time: 5 Minutes
Ingredients:
- 1 cup freshly squeezed orange juice
- 1 cup mango, copped
- 2 kiwi fruits, peeled and chopped
- ½ cup arugula
- ½ cup ice berg lettuce
- 1 cup fresh kale, stems removed and chopped
- 1 teaspoon flax seed powder
- 3-4 ice cubes

Directions:
1. Place all the ingredients in the blender and process until your desired consistency has reached.

Nutrition Info: (Per Serving): Calories- 350, Fat- 2 g, Protein- 7g, Carbohydrates- 85 g

Ginger- Parsely Grape Smoothie

Servings: 1
Cooking Time: 2 Minutes
Ingredients:
- 1 ½ cup red grapes, seedless

- ½ cup parsley, washed and chopped
- 2 tablespoons avocado flesh
- ¼ cup freshly squeezed lemon juice
- 1 teaspoon freshly grated ginger
- 3 drops of liquid Stevia or ½ teaspoon raw organic honey
- 4-5 mint leaves
- A handful of ice cubes

Directions:
1. Add all the ingredients into the blender and blitz until smooth.

Nutrition Info: (Per Serving): Calories- 230, Fat- 5.4 g, Protein- 3.9 g, Carbohydrates- 55 g

SUPERFOOD SMOOTHIES

Coconut Blue Wonder

Servings: 2
Cooking Time: 5 Minutes
Ingredients:
- 1 cup whole blueberries (fresh or frozen)
- 1 cup organic coconut milk
- ¼ cup plain low fat yogurt
- 1 small handful of baby spinach, chopped
- 1 ½ teaspoon flaxseed powder
- 3-4 ice cubes

Directions:
1. Combine all the ingredients in a blender jar and run it for 1 minute or until smooth and creamy.

Nutrition Info: (Per Serving): Calories- 240, Fat- 11 g, Protein- 4 g, Carbohydrates- 31 g

Carrot Crunch Smoothie

Servings: 2
Cooking Time: 5 Minutes
Ingredients:
- 1 grapefruit, peeled and seeded
- 1 cup carrot, peeled and chopped
- 1 cup low fat plain yogurt
- 2 teaspoons raw, organic honey
- 3 teaspoons macadamia nuts, chopped
- 3 teaspoons almonds, chopped
- 5-6 ice cubes

Directions:
1. Place all the ingredients into the high speed blender jar and run it on high for 20 seconds until everything is well combined. Pour into serving glass and enjoy!

Nutrition Info: (Per Serving): Calories- 310, Fat- 12 g, Protein- 11 g, Carbohydrates- 39 g

Blackberry Mango Crunch

Servings: 3
Cooking Time: 2 Minutes
Ingredients:
- 1 ripe banana, peeled and chopped
- 1 pear, cored and chopped
- ¼ cup whole blackberries (fresh or frozen)
- ¼ cup cashews
- 1 teaspoon maqui berry powder
- 8-9 fresh mint leaves
- 2 teaspoons freshly squeezed lemon juice
- 1 cup filtered water

- 4-5 ice cubes

Directions:

1. Combine all the ingredients in a blender jar and run it for 1 minute or until smooth and creamy.

Nutrition Info: (Per Serving): Calories- 200, Fat- 6.4 g, Protein- 3.1 g, Carbohydrates- 35 g

Berry Melon Green Smoothie

Servings: 3
Cooking Time: 5 Minutes

Ingredients:

- ¾ cup watermelon, chopped
- ½ cup whole strawberries (fresh or frozen)
- 1 ½ cup fresh baby spinach, washed and chopped
- 1 ripe banana, chopped
- 1 cup fresh coconut water
- Freshly squeezed juice of ½ lime
- 1 ½ teaspoon flaxseed powder
- 3-4 ice cubes

Directions:

1. Add all the ingredients in the same order as listed above and blend until smooth and thick

Nutrition Info: (Per Serving): Calories- 121, Fat- 1.5 g, Protein- 3 g, Carbohydrates- 25 g

Green Tea Superfood Smooothie

Servings: 4
Cooking Time: 5 Minutes

Ingredients:

- ½ cup freshly prepared pomegranate juice
- 1 cup freshly brewed green tea (unsweetened and chilled)
- ½ cup plain low fat Greek yogurt
- 1 cup mixed berries (fresh or frozen)
- 1 ripe banana, chopped (fresh or frozen)
- 1 large handful baby spinach, washed and chopped
- 1 teaspoon freshly grated ginger
- 1 teaspoon flaxseed powder
- 3-4 ice cubes

Directions:

1. To make this smoothie, add all the ingredients into your high speed blender and puree until smooth.

Nutrition Info: (Per Serving): Calories-130, Fat- 1 g, Protein- 6.9 g, Carbohydrates- 27 g

Tea And Grape Smoothie

Servings: 2
Cooking Time: 5 Minutes

Ingredients:
- 1 large apple, cored and chopped
- 1 cup red grapes, seedless
- ½ cup freshly brewed green tea (unsweetened and chilled)
- ½ cup plain low fat yogurt
- 1 teaspoons raw organic honey
- 1 teaspoons freshly grated ginger
- 3-4 ice cubes

Directions:
1. Load your high speed blender jar with all the ingredients and puree until thick and smooth.

Nutrition Info: (Per Serving): Calories- 131, Fat- 1 g, Protein- 5 g, Carbohydrates- 25 g

Super Tropi-kale Wonder

Servings: 4
Cooking Time: 5 Minutes
Ingredients:
- 1 cup pineapple, chopped
- 1 cup mango, peeled and hopped
- 2 cups mixed greens, washed and chopped
- 1 ripe banana, chopped
- 1 teaspoon Spirulina powder
- ½ teaspoon bee pollen
- 3 teaspoons Brazil nuts
- 2 teaspoons flax seeds
- 1 ½ teaspoon pure coconut oil
- 1 ¼ cup filtered water
- 3-4 ice cubes

Directions:
1. Add all the ingredients in the same order as listed above and blend until smooth and thick.

Nutrition Info: (Per Serving): Calories- 300, Fat-11 g, Protein-7.4 g, Carbohydrates-45 g

Nutty Mango Green Blend

Servings: 2
Cooking Time: 5 Minutes
Ingredients:
- 1 cup fresh mango, chopped (fresh or frozen)
- 1 cup fresh baby spinach, washed and chopped
- ½ cup low fat plain yogurt
- 1 teaspoon pistachios
- 1 teaspoon peanuts
- 1 teaspoon pecan nuts
- ½ teaspoon liquid Stevia
- 2 teaspoons freshly squeezed lemon juice
- 5 ice cubes

Directions:
1.   To you blender, add the above ingredient and pulse until smooth.
Nutrition Info: (Per Serving): Calories-300, Fat- 6.8 g, Protein- 12 g, Carbohydrates- 45 g

Basil- Bee Pollen Chlorella Smoothie

Servings: 2-3
Cooking Time: 5 Minutes
Ingredients:
- ½ cup pineapple, peeled and chopped
- 1 cup fresh coconut water
- 2 tablespoon ripe avocado flesh
- 1/3 cup low fat plain yogurt
- 1 teaspoon cacao powder
- 2 teaspoon coconut flakes
- 1 teaspoon raw organic honey
- 1 teaspoon bee pollen
- 1 teaspoon Chia seeds
- 1 teaspoon chlorella
- 1 teaspoon maca root powder
- 1 teaspoon freshly squeezed lemon juice
- 5-6 fresh basil leaves
- 1 teaspoon freshly squeezed lemon juice
- A pinch of Himalayan salt
- 4-5 ice cubes

Directions:
1.   In a blender, combine all the above listed ingredients and blend until nice and smooth.
Nutrition Info: (Per Serving): Calories- 320, Fat- 14 g, Protein- 14 g, Carbohydrates- 40 g

Hemp, Date And Chia Smoothie

Servings: 2
Cooking Time: 2 Minutes
Ingredients:
- 1 cup unsweetened almond milk
- ¼ teaspoon vanilla extract
- 1 dates, pitted
- 1 tablespoon hemp seeds
- ½ ripe banana, chopped
- 1 teaspoon Chia seeds, soaked
- A large handful of chopped kale
- 4-5 ice cubes

Directions:
1.   Place all the ingredients into your blender and run it on medium high speed for 1-2 minutes or until done.
Nutrition Info: (Per Serving): Calories- 218, Fat- 11 g, Protein- 8 g, Carbohydrates- 31 g

Chia Berry Spinach Smoothie

Servings: 2
Cooking Time: 2 Minutes
Ingredients:
- ½ cup whole strawberries (fresh or frozen)
- ½ cup whole blueberry (fresh or frozen)
- 1 cup baby spinach, washed and chopped
- ½ cup low fat plain yogurt
- ¼ teaspoons cinnamon powder
- 3 teaspoons Chia seeds, soaked
- 1 teaspoons flaxseed powder
- ½ teaspoons liquid Stevia or 1 teaspoon raw organic honey
- 4-5 ice cubes

Directions:
1. Pour all the ingredients into your blender and whizz it up till the desired consistency is reached.

Nutrition Info: (Per Serving): Calories- 228, Fat- 4 g, Protein- 10 g, Carbohydrates- 35 g

Blue And Green Wonder

Servings: 3
Cooking Time: 5 Minutes
Ingredients:
- 1 cup unsweetened almond milk
- 1 cup whole blueberries (fresh or frozen)
- 1 ripe banana, chopped
- 1 cup baby spinach, washed and chopped
- 1 cup fresh kale, stems removed and chopped
- 2 teaspoons flax seeds
- 4-5 ice cubes

Directions:
1. Add all the ingredients in the same order as listed above and blend until smooth and thick

Nutrition Info: (Per Serving): Calories- 122, Fat- 2 g, Protein- 3 g, Carbohydrates- 25 g

Choco- Berry Delight

Servings: 4
Cooking Time: 5 Minutes
Ingredients:
- ½ cup whole blueberries (fresh or frozen)
- ½ cup cherries, pitted
- 1 ripe banana, chopped
- 1 cup unsweetened almond milk
- 2 cups mixed greens, washed and chopped
- 1 cup baby spinach, washed and chopped
- 2 stalks celery, copped

- 2 teaspoons raw cacao powder
- 1teapoon Chia seeds
- 3-4 ice cubes

Directions:

1. Place all the ingredients into your blender and run it on medium high speed for 1-2 minutes or until done.

Nutrition Info: (Per Serving): Calories- 310, Fat- 7.9 g, Protein- 8 g, Carbohydrates- 59 g

Green Chia Smoothie

Servings: 3
Cooking Time: 5 Minutes

Ingredients:

- 1 ½ cups spinach, washed and chopped
- 1 large kale leaf, chopped
- 1 cup English cucumber, chopped
- 1 small apple, cored and chopped
- 1 teaspoon freshly squeezed lemon juice
- 3 teaspoons Chia seeds, soaked
- 1 teaspoon raw organic honey
- 1 ½ cup filtered water
- 3-4 ice cubes

Directions:

1. To you blender, add the above ingredient and pulse until smooth.

Nutrition Info: (Per Serving): Calories- 100, Fat- 2.9 g, Protein- 5 g, Carbohydrates- 18.5 g

GREEN SMOOTHIES

Berry Spinach Basil Smoothie

Servings: 2
Cooking Time: 5 Minutes
Ingredients:
- 1 cup unsweetened almond milk
- 1 small banana, chopped
- ½ cup blueberries (fresh or frozen)
- A small handful of baby spinach
- 6-7 fresh basil leaves
- 2 teaspoons freshly squeezed lemon juice
- 3-4 ice cubes

Directions:
1. Add all the ingredients into the high speed blender and whizz until smooth.

Nutrition Info: (Per Serving): Calories- 250, Fat- 5.8g, Protein- 5 g ,Carbohydrates- 51 g

Clementine Green Smoothie

Servings: 3
Cooking Time: 5 Minutes
Ingredients:
- 2-3 Clementine, peeled and deseeded
- 1 small banana, chopped
- ¼ cup fresh coconut milk
- 1 small handful of mixed greens
- A few sprigs of mint leaves
- A few fresh cilantro leaves
- ½ teaspoon raw organic honey
- 1 teaspoon freshly squeezed lemon juice
- 3-4 ice cubes

Directions:
1. Add all the ingredients into the high speed blender and whizz until smooth.

Nutrition Info: (Per Serving): Calories- 180, Fat- 3.2 g, Protein- 3.5 g, Carbohydrates- 42 g

Lovely Green Gazpacho

Servings: 2
Cooking Time: 5 Minutes
Ingredients:
- ½ cup ice
- 1 cup collard greens, chopped
- ¼ cup red bell pepper, diced
- ½ cup frozen broccoli florets
- ½ cup fresh tomatoes, chopped
- 1 garlic clove

- ¼ cup fresh cilantro, chopped
- ½ lemon, juiced
- ½ cup water

Directions:
1. Add all the ingredients except vegetables/fruits first
2. Blend until smooth
3. Add the vegetable/fruits
4. Blend until smooth
5. Add a few ice cubes and serve the smoothie
6. Enjoy!

Nutrition Info: Calories: 70; Fat: 1g; Carbohydrates: 13g; Protein: 4g

A Peachy Medley

Servings: 2
Cooking Time: 5 Minutes
Ingredients:
- 1 cup coconut water
- 1 tablespoon flaxseed, ground
- 1 scoop vanilla protein powder
- ¼ cup frozen peaches
- ½ cup frozen tart cherries
- 1 cup dandelion greens, chopped

Directions:
1. Add all the ingredients except vegetables/fruits first
2. Blend until smooth
3. Add the vegetable/fruits
4. Blend until smooth
5. Add a few ice cubes and serve the smoothie
6. Enjoy!

Nutrition Info: Calories: 300; Fat: 7g; Carbohydrates: 45g; Protein: 32g

Date And Apricot Green Smoothie

Servings: 2 Large
Cooking Time: 2 Minutes
Ingredients:
- ¾ cup unsweetened almond milk
- 1 small apricot, pitted and chopped
- 1 medjool dates, pitted
- 1 small banana, chopped
- ½ cup kale, stems removed and chopped
- ½ cup baby spinach, washed
- A handful of mixed berries
- Few ice cubes

Directions:
1. Pour the ingredients into the blender and process until smooth.

Nutrition Info: (Per Serving): Calories- 202, Fat- 3.6 g, Protein- 7.6 g, Carbohydrates- 38 g

Tropical Matcha Kale

Servings: 2
Cooking Time: 5 Minutes
Ingredients:
- ½ cup ice
- 1 cup kale, chopped
- ½ cup frozen mango died
- 1 teaspoon matcha powder
- ½ cup plain kefir
- ¼ cup cold water

Directions:
1. Add all the ingredients except vegetables/fruits first
2. Blend until smooth
3. Add the vegetable/fruits
4. Blend until smooth
5. Add a few ice cubes and serve the smoothie
6. Enjoy!

Nutrition Info: Calories: 126; Fat: 2g; Carbohydrates: 23g; Protein: 6g

The Green Potato Chai

Servings: 2
Cooking Time: 5 Minutes
Ingredients:
- ½ cup chilled, brewed chai
- ½ cup ice
- 1½ cups kale, chopped
- 1 pear, roughly chopped
- 1 scoop unsweetened protein powder
- ¼ teaspoon cinnamon

Directions:
1. Add all the ingredients except vegetables/fruits first
2. Blend until smooth
3. Add the vegetable/fruits
4. Blend until smooth
5. Add a few ice cubes and serve the smoothie
6. Enjoy!

Nutrition Info: Calories: 286; Fat: 1g; Carbohydrates: 43g; Protein: 29g

The Deep Green Lagoon

Servings: 2
Cooking Time: 5 Minutes
Ingredients:

- ½ cup ice
- ½ cup collard greens, chopped
- 1 cup spinach, chopped
- ½ cup fresh broccoli florets, diced
- 1 pear, roughly chopped
- 1 teaspoon spirulina powder
- ½ cup of water

Directions:
1. Add all the ingredients except vegetables/fruits first
2. Blend until smooth
3. Add the vegetable/fruits
4. Blend until smooth
5. Add a few ice cubes and serve the smoothie
6. Enjoy!

Nutrition Info: Calories: 124; Fat: 1g; Carbohydrates: 30g; Protein: 4g

Lemon Cilantro Delight

Servings: 2
Cooking Time: 5 Minutes
Ingredients:
- ½ cup ice
- 1 cup dandelion greens, chopped
- 2 celery stalks, roughly chopped
- 1 pear, roughly chopped
- 1 tablespoon chia seeds
- ¼ cup fresh cilantro, chopped
- Juice of ½ lemon
- ¼ cup water

Directions:
1. Add all the ingredients except vegetables/fruits first
2. Blend until smooth
3. Add the vegetable/fruits
4. Blend until smooth
5. Add a few ice cubes and serve the smoothie
6. Enjoy!

Nutrition Info: Calories: 200; Fat: 5g; Carbohydrates: 34g; Protein: 5g

Pineapple And Cucumber Cooler

Servings: 3-4
Cooking Time: 5 Minutes
Ingredients:
- 1 green apple, cored and chopped
- 1 cup pineapple, peeled and chopped
- 1 green cucumber, deseeded and chopped
- 5-6 celery stalks, chopped

- A handful of kale leaves, stems removed and chopped
- 1/3 cup fresh parsley
- 1 teaspoon freshly grated ginger
- 1 tablespoon freshly squeezed lemon juice
- 3-4 ice cubes

Directions:
1. Add all the ingredients into the blender jar and pulse it on high for 30 seconds or until smooth.

Nutrition Info: (Per Serving): Calories-226, Fat- 1.8 g, Protein- 7.8 g, Carbohydrates- 36 g

Passion Green Smoothie

Servings: 2
Cooking Time: 10 Minutes
Ingredients:
- 1 cup strawberries
- 2 cups spinach, raw
- ½ cup blueberries
- ½ cup Greek yogurt
- 2 cups of water

Directions:
1. Add listed ingredients to a blender
2. Blend until you have a smooth and creamy texture
3. Serve chilled and enjoy!

Nutrition Info: Calories: 88; Fat: 1.5g; Carbohydrates: 13.9g; Protein: 6.6g

The Curious Raspberry And Green Shake

Servings: 1
Cooking Time: 10 Minutes
Ingredients:
- ¼ cup raspberry
- 1 tablespoon macadamia oil
- 1 cup whole milk
- 1 pack stevia
- 1 cup spinach
- 1 cup of water

Directions:
1. Add listed ingredients to a blender
2. Blend until you get a smooth and creamy texture
3. Serve chilled and enjoy!

Nutrition Info: Calories: 292; Fat: 21g; Carbohydrates: 17g; Protein: 9g

Dandellion Green Berry Smoothie

Servings: 2
Cooking Time: 5 Minutes

Ingredients:
- ½ cup dandelion greens, chopped
- ½ small banana, hopped
- A handful of mixed berries
- 1 cup filtered water
- 1 teaspoon coconut oil
- A pinch of cinnamon powder
- 1 teaspoon flax seed powder
- 1 teaspoon cacao powder
- 1 teaspoon raw organic honey
- ½ teaspoon Chia seeds
- ½ teaspoon hemp seeds
- 3-4 ice cubes

Directions:
1. Add all the above listed ingredients into your blender, secure the lid and blitz until smooth.

Nutrition Info: (Per Serving): Calories- 270, Fat- 16 g, Protein- 3.2 g, Carbohydrates- 35 g

Glowing Green Smoothie

Servings: 2
Cooking Time: 10 Minutes

Ingredients:
- 2 bananas
- 2 kiwis
- 4 celery stalks
- ½ cup pineapple
- 2 cups of water
- 4 cups spinach

Directions:
1. Add all the listed ingredients to a blender
2. Blend until you have a smooth and creamy texture
3. Serve chilled and enjoy!

Nutrition Info: Calories: 191; Fat: 1.1g; Carbohydrates: 46.5g; Protein: 7.8g

VEGAN AND VEGETARIAN DIET SMOOTHIES

Beet And Grapefruit Smoothie

Servings: 1
Cooking Time: 5 Min
Ingredients:
- 1/2 Cucumber, peeled and diced
- 1/2 small red beet, peeled and diced
- 1 apple, cored and chopped
- 6 tbsps. Grapefruit juice
- 4 ice cubes

Directions:
1. In a high speed blender, add cucumber and blend until it breaks into pieces. Add apple, beet and blend until smooth.
2. Add water if it's too hard to blend. Push the sides and blend again until you reach fine consistency. Add ice, grapefruit juice and blend.
3. Serve right away.

Nutrition Info: (Per Serving): Cal 208 Total Fat 1.2 g, Carbs 45.9 g, Fiber 4 g, Protein 6 g, Sodium 33 mg Sugars 25 g

Avocado And Blueberry Smoothie

Servings: 2
Cooking Time: 10 Min
Ingredients:
- 1 cup orange juice
- 1/2 cup mineral water
- 1 haas avocado, seeded and peeled
- 1 cup fresh blueberries
- 1/4 cup vegan yogurt
- 1 tbsp. maple syrup
- 1 cup frozen blueberries
- 1/2 cup frozen raspberries
- 1/4 cup fresh mint leaves
- Pinch of Celtic salt

Directions:
1. Throw everything in a high speed blender. Process until smooth.
2. Serve right away.

Nutrition Info: (Per Serving): Cal 111 Total Fat 12.3 g, Carbs 39.2 g, Fiber 8.1 g, Protein 11 g, Sodium 206 mg Sugars 29 g

Apple, Carrot, Ginger & Fennel Smoothie

Servings: 2
Cooking Time: 5 Min
Ingredients:
- 1 medium apple

- 2 medium carrots
- 2 tablespoons peeled ginger slices
- 1 cup sliced fennel bulb
- 1 tablespoon honey
- 1 cup apple juice
- 1 tablespoons lemon juice
- 1 cup ice cubes

Directions:
1. Peel and core apple, cut into slices and place in a blender.
2. Peel carrots, dice and add to blender along with ginger, fennel bulb, honey, apple juice, lemon juice and ice cubes.
3. Pulse for 1 minute until smoothie and serve immediately.

Nutrition Info: (Per Serving):144 Cal, 0 g total fat (0 g sat. fat), 0 mg chol., 63 mg sodium, 36 g carb., 5g fiber, 2 g protein.

Mango, Lime & Spinach Smoothie

Servings: 2
Cooking Time: 5 Min
Ingredients:
- 1 cup seedless green grapes
- 2 cups baby spinach
- 1 large Mango
- 2 tablespoons lime juice
- 1 cup ice cubes

Directions:
1. Peel and core mango, roughly chop flesh and place in a blender.
2. Add grapes, spinach, lime juice, ice and pulse for 1 minute until smooth.
3. Serve immediately.

Nutrition Info: (Per Serving):167 Cal, 0 g total fat (0 g sat. fat), 0 mg chol., 67 mg sodium, 64 g carb., 5g fiber, 6 g protein.

Chard, Lime & Mint Smoothies

Servings: 2
Cooking Time: 5 Min
Ingredients:
- 5 ½ ounces honeydew melon
- 3 ounces kiwifruit
- 2 cups green Swiss chards
- ½ cup soda, lime-flavored
- ¼ cup chopped mint
- 3 tablespoons reduced fat vanilla milk
- ⅛ Teaspoon salt
- 3 tablespoons lime juice
- 1 cup ice cubes

Directions:

1. Peel and core melon, cut into cubes and place in a blender.
2. Peel and core kiwifruit and add to melon along with soda, mint and milk.
3. Remove stems of chards, discard, discard leaves into strips and add to blender.
4. Add ice and pulse for 1 minute until smooth. Add more lime juice if smoothie is thick.
5. Serve immediately.

Nutrition Info: (Per Serving):67 Cal, 0.7 g total fat (0 g sat. fat), 0 mg chol., 267 mg sodium, 16 g carb., 3g fiber, 2 g protein.

Healthy Kiwi Smoothie

Servings: 2
Cooking Time: 20 Min
Ingredients:
- 1 celery stalk
- 2 medium granny smith apples, cored
- 1 kiwi fruit, peeled and chopped
- 1/3 cup parsley leaves
- 1 tbsp. grated ginger
- Maple syrup
- 2 tsp lime juice

Directions:
1. Add all ingredients in a blender, except lime juice and blend until smooth. Taste and adjust sweetness with maple syrup.
2. Stir in lime juice and serve.

Nutrition Info: (Per Serving): Cal 82 Total Fat 1 g, Carbs 20 g, Fiber 0 g, Protein 1 g, Sodium 9 mg Sugars 18 g

Spinach, Grape, & Coconut Smoothie

Servings: 2
Cooking Time: 5 Min
Ingredients:
- 2 cups seedless green grapes
- 2 cups baby spinach
- ½ cup reduced fat coconut milk
- 1 cup ice cubes

Directions:
1. In a blender, place grapes, spinach and ice, and pour in milk.
2. Pulse for 1 minute until smooth and serve immediately.

Nutrition Info: (Per Serving):194 Cal, 2 g total fat (0 g sat. fat), 0 mg chol., 108 mg sodium, 31 g carb., 4g fiber, 0 g protein.

Green Smoothie

Servings: 2
Cooking Time: 5 Min
Ingredients:

- 2 medium green apples
- Half of a medium avocado
- 1-inch ginger piece
- 1 cup baby spinach
- 1 cup coconut water
- 1 tablespoon flax oil
- 1 cup ice cubes

Directions:
1. Peel apple, core, slice and place in a blender. Peel and pit avocado and add to blender.
2. Peel and dice ginger and add to blender along with spinach, coconut water, flax oil and ice cubes.
3. Pulse for 1 minute until smooth and creamy and then serve over ice.

Nutrition Info: (Per Serving):156 Cal, 1 g total fat (0.2 g sat. fat), 0 mg chol., 54 mg sodium, 38 g carb., 6.5g fiber, 3.6 g protein.

Super Avocado Smoothie

Servings: 2
Cooking Time: 5 Min
Ingredients:
- 1 medium avocado
- 1 cup blueberries
- 1 cup frozen strawberries
- ½ cup frozen raspberries
- ¼ cup reduced fat vanilla yogurt
- 1 cup orange juice
- ½ cup filtered water
- 1 tablespoon maple syrup
- 15 mint leaves

Directions:
1. Peel and pit avocado and add to a blender.
2. Add blueberries, strawberries, raspberries, yogurt, orange juice, water, maple syrup and mint.
3. Pulse for 1 minute until smooth and serve immediately.

Nutrition Info: (Per Serving):156 Cal, 8 g total fat (1 g sat. fat), 0 mg chol., 64 mg sodium, 54 g carb., 8g fiber, 3 g protein.

Strawberry Watermelon Smoothie

Servings: 2
Cooking Time: 5 Min
Ingredients:
- 1 1/2 cups sliced watermelons, seeds removed
- 1 cup frozen strawberries
- 1/2 frozen ripe banana, sliced
- 1/2 cup unsweetened almond milk
- 1 lime juice

- 1 tbsp. chia seeds

Directions:

1. Add all ingredients in a blender. Process until smooth and fine texture. Adjust sweetness with more banana.
2. Top with more chia seeds.

Nutrition Info: (Per Serving): Cal 182 Total Fat 6.2 g, Carbs 30 g, Fiber 9 g, Protein 5 g, Sodium 48 mg Sugars 14 g

Chai Tea Smoothie

Servings: 2
Cooking Time: 10 Min

Ingredients:

- 1 cup unsweetened almond milk
- 1 cup coconut juice
- 1/4 cup chopped dates, soaked
- 1 tsp vanilla extract
- 1/2 tsp cinnamon powder
- 1/4 tsp ginger powder
- 1/8 tsp nutmeg powder
- 1/8 tsp cardamom powder
- Pinch of cloves powder
- Pinch of Himalayan sea salt
- 2 large frozen bananas, sliced
- 1 cup crushed ice
- 1 tbsp. chia seeds

Directions:

1. Add everything in a high-speed blender. Blend until smooth and creamy.
2. Serve right away!

Nutrition Info: (Per Serving): Cal 227 Total Fat 1 g, Carbs 52 g, Fiber 6 g, Protein 3 g, Sodium 280 mg Sugars 35 g

Mango Smoothie

Servings: 2
Cooking Time: 5 Min

Ingredients:

- 1 1/2 cups orange juice
- 1/2 cup water
- 1/4 cup sliced avocado
- 1/2 tsp lime zest, grated
- 2 cups frozen sweet mango
- 1 tsp maple syrup

Directions:

1. Place all the ingredients in a blender. Blend until smooth and fine texture. Add more water if too thick and blend again.
2. To adjust sweetness, add more maple syrup. Enjoy while still cold!

Nutrition Info: (Per Serving): Cal 270 Total Fat 1.5 g, Carbs 53 g, Fiber 6 g, Protein 16 g, Sodium 0 mg Sugars 37 g

Lime & Green Tea Smoothie Bowl

Servings: 2
Cooking Time: 10 Min
Ingredients:
- 1/2 cup coconut juice/ water
- 1 cup fresh spinach leaves
- 1 large frozen banana slices
- 1/4 cup avocado slices
- 2 tsp lime zest
- 1 tbsp. and 1 tsp lime juice
- 3 ice cubes
- 2 tsp maple syrup
- 1/2 tsp good quality Matcha Green Tea powder
- Toppings:
- Granola, chopped into pieces
- Coconut flakes
- Coconut cream

Directions:
1. Put all the ingredients in a high-speed blender, except the toppings. Blend until smooth.
2. Transfer in glasses or bowls. Put toppings as much as you want. Enjoy!

Nutrition Info: (Per Serving): Cal 437 Total Fat 22.4 g, Carbs 55.4 g, Fiber 10.9 g, Protein 10.4 g, Sodium 44 mg Sugars 31.9 g

Chia, Blueberry & Banana Smoothie

Servings: 2
Cooking Time: 5 Min
Ingredients:
- 2 medium fresh bananas
- 1 cup frozen blueberries
- 1 cup fat free milk, unsweetened
- 2 tablespoons Chia Seeds
- 1 cup ice cubes

Directions:
1. Peel banana, chop roughly and place in a blender along with blueberries, milk, chia seeds and ice.
2. Pulse 1 minute until smooth and serve immediately.

Nutrition Info: (Per Serving):220 Cal, 1.5 g total fat (0.5 g sat. fat), 0 mg chol., 71 mg sodium, 48 g carb., 3.4g fiber, 5.5 g protein.

BRAIN HEALTH SMOOTHIES

Buddha's Banana Berry

Servings: 2
Cooking Time: 5 Minutes
Ingredients:
- 1 tablespoon hemp seeds
- ¾ cup plain low-fat Greek yogurt
- 1 fresh banana
- 1 cup baby spinach
- 1 cup frozen raspberries
- 1 cup unsweetened vanilla almond milk

Directions:
1. Add all the ingredients except vegetables/fruits first
2. Blend until smooth
3. Add the vegetable/fruits
4. Blend until smooth
5. Add a few ice cubes and serve the smoothie
6. Enjoy!

Nutrition Info: Calories: 205; Fat: 1g; Carbohydrates: 51g; Protein: 3g

Hale 'n' Kale Banana Smoothie

Servings: 1
Cooking Time: 2 Minutes
Ingredients:
- 1 cup fresh kale, chopped (stems removed)
- 1 handful blueberries (fresh or frozen)
- 1 small banana, chopped (fresh or frozen)
- ½ teaspoon Chia seeds
- ½ cup filtered water

Directions:
1. Add the kale, berries, banana, Chia seeds and water into your blender jar and process on high for 20 seconds or until smooth and frothy.

Nutrition Info: (Per Serving): Calories- 201, Fat- 1.2 g, Protein- 3.9 g, Carbohydrates- 44 g

Chia-hemp Berry Smoothie

Servings: 2
Cooking Time: 5 Minutes
Ingredients:
- 1 cup unsweetened almond milk
- 1 cup whole strawberries (fresh or frozen)
- ¼ cup blueberries (fresh or frozen)
- ¼ cup raspberries (fresh or frozen)
- ¼ cup lack berries 9fresh or frozen)
- ¼ cup cranberries 9fresh or frozen)

- 3 tablespoons chopped almonds
- 3 teaspoons almond butter
- 3 teaspoons hemp seeds
- 2 teaspoons Chia seeds, soaked

Directions:

1. Place the ingredients into the blender, secure the lid and blend until the smoothie is nice and thick.

Nutrition Info: (Per Serving): Calories- 266, Fat- 17.8 g, Protein- 7 g, Carbohydrates- 26.3 g

Beet-berry Brain Booster

Servings: 2
Cooking Time: 5 Minutes
Ingredients:

- 1/3 cup apple, cored and chopped
- ½ cup raw red beet, peeled and chopped
- 1 cup carrots, peeled and chopped
- ½ cup blueberries (fresh or frozen)
- 1 teaspoon freshly squeezed lemon juice
- 1/3 cup unsalted almonds
- ½ teaspoon freshly grated ginger
- 1 teaspoon raw organic honey
- A handful of ice cubes

Directions:

1. Load your blender with the ingredient listed above and process on medium high for 30 seconds or until done. Serve immediately.

Nutrition Info: (Per Serving): Calories- 322, Fat- 8 g, Protein- 11 g, Carbohydrates- 36 g

3 Spice-almond Smoothie

Servings: 1 Large
Cooking Time: 5 Minutes
Ingredients:

- ¾ cup unsweetened almond milk
- 1 banana, sliced (fresh or frozen)
- A handful of fresh kale, stems removed
- 1 teaspoon almond butter
- A pinch of nutmeg powder
- 1 pinch of cinnamon powder
- ¼ teaspoon of freshly grated ginger
- ½ teaspoon of raw organic honey

Directions:

1. Place all the ingredients into the high speed blender jar and run it on high for 20 seconds until everything is well combined. Pour into serving glass and enjoy!

Nutrition Info: (Per Serving): Calories- 238, Fat- 10 g, Protein- 5.5 g, Carbohydrates- 39 g

Orange- Broccoli Green Monster

Servings: 2
Cooking Time: 5 Minutes
Ingredients:
- ½ cup chopped carrot
- ½ cup freshly squeezed orange juice
- A large handful of fresh kale, stems removed
- 1 large apple, cored and chopped
- 1 cup tightly packed baby spinach
- 1 banana, chopped (fresh or frozen)
- 1 handful of broccoli florets
- 1 tablespoon freshly squeeze lemon juice

Directions:
1. Load your blender jar with all the ingredients listed above and whizz until smooth and frothy.

Nutrition Info: (Per Serving): Calories- 255, Fat- 1.5 g, Protein- 5.2 g, Carbohydrates- 65 g

Rosemary And Lemon Garden Smoothie

Servings: 1
Cooking Time: 10 Minutes
Ingredients:
- 1 stalk fresh rosemary
- 1 tablespoon lemon juice, fresh
- ½ cup whole milk yogurt
- 1 cup garden greens
- 1 tablespoon pepitas
- 1 tablespoon olive oil
- 1 tablespoon flaxseed, ground
- 1 pack stevia
- 1 ½ cups of water

Directions:
1. Add listed ingredients to a blender
2. Blend until you get a smooth and creamy texture
3. Serve chilled and enjoy!

Nutrition Info: Calories: 312; Fat: 25g; Carbohydrates: 14g; Protein: 9g

The Blueberry Bliss

Servings: 1
Cooking Time: 10 Minutes
Ingredients:
- ¼ cup frozen blueberries, unsweetened
- 16 ounces unsweetened almond milk, vanilla
- 4 ounces heavy cream
- 1 scoop vanilla whey protein

- 1 pack stevia

Directions:
1. Add listed ingredients to a blender
2. Blend until you have a smooth and creamy texture
3. Serve chilled and enjoy!

Nutrition Info: Calories: 302; Fat: 25g; Carbohydrates: 4g; Protein: 15g

Cinnammon-apple Green Smoothie

Servings: 2
Cooking Time: 5 Minutes
Ingredients:
- ¾ cup unsweetened almond milk
- 1 cup fresh kale, stems removed
- 1 cup baby spinach, washed and chopped
- 1 large apple, peeled, cored and chopped
- 1 large banana, chopped (fresh or frozen)
- 1 teaspoon raw, organic honey
- ½ teaspoon cinnamon powder
- 3-4 ice cubes

Directions:
1. To your blender jar, add all the above mentioned ingredients and process until smooth.

Nutrition Info: (Per Serving): Calories-243, Fat- 3.2 g, Protein- 4.5 g, Carbohydrates- 47 g

Sweet Pea Smoothie

Servings: 2
Cooking Time: 10 Minutes
Ingredients:
- 2 cups sweet peas
- 1 cup blueberries
- 1 teaspoon honey
- 2 bananas
- 2 cups almond milk
- 2 tablespoons chia seeds

Directions:
1. Add all the listed ingredients to a blender
2. Blend until you have a smooth and creamy texture
3. Serve chilled and enjoy!

Nutrition Info: Calories: 202; Fat: 4.1g; Carbohydrates: 38.4g; Protein: 6.8g

Cacao-goji Berry Marvel

Servings: 2 Small
Cooking Time: 5 Minutes
Ingredients:
- 1 cup unsweetened almond milk

- 1 large banana, chopped (preferably frozen)
- ¼ cup Goji berries
- 3-4 fresh kale leaves, stems removed
- 1 ½ teaspoon cacao powder
- 3 teaspoon almond butter
- ¼ teaspoon cinnamon powder
- 4-6 ice cubes

Directions:
1. Load your blender with all the smoothie ingredients and process it on medium speed until the smoothie is ready. Serve immediately.

Nutrition Info: (Per Serving): Calories- 345, Fat- 10 g, Protein- 12 g, Carbohydrates- 57 g

Brain Nutrition-analyzer

Servings: 2
Cooking Time: 5 Minutes
Ingredients:
- 4 large ice cubes
- ¾ cup plain-low-fat Greek yogurt
- 1 cup baby spinach
- 1 cup unsweetened vanilla almond milk
- 2 fresh bananas
- 1 tablespoon almond butter
- 1 tablespoon peanut butter

Directions:
1. Add all the ingredients except vegetables/fruits first
2. Blend until smooth
3. Add the vegetable/fruits
4. Blend until smooth
5. Add a few ice cubes and serve the smoothie
6. Enjoy!

Nutrition Info: Calories: 147; Fat: 7g; Carbohydrates: 21g; Protein: 4g

Cucumber Kiwi Crush

Servings: 2
Cooking Time: 5 Minutes
Ingredients:
- 1 cup green cucumber, roughly chopped
- 1 large kiwi, peeled and chopped
- ½ cp plain low fat yogurt
- ½ cup freshly prepared tangerine juice
- 1 cup fresh baby spinach, washed and chopped
- ½ avocado, peeled and chopped
- 1 teaspoon of freshly squeezed lemon juice
- A small handful of mint leaves
- A handful of ice cubes

Directions:
1. Combine all the ingredients in the blender and process until there are no lumps. Serve immediately.
Nutrition Info: (Per Serving): Calories-185, Fat- 7.8 g, Protein- 5.2 g, Carbohydrates- 32 g

Brewed Green Tea Smoothie

Servings: 4
Cooking Time: 10 Minutes
Ingredients:
- 2 large avocados, pitted and peeled
- 4 cups spinach
- ½ cup fresh mint leaves
- 2 cups green tea, brewed and cooled
- 4 stalks celery, chopped
- 2 grapefruits, peeled and frozen
- 4 cups pineapple, chunked and frozen
- ¼ teaspoon ground cayenne pepper

Directions:
1. Add all the listed ingredients to a blender
2. Blend until you have a smooth and creamy texture
3. Serve chilled and enjoy!
Nutrition Info: Calories: 155; Fat: 0.4g; Carbohydrates: 8g; Protein: 5.6g

BEAUTY SMOOTHIES

Chocolaty Berry Blast

Servings: 2
Cooking Time: 2 Minutes
Ingredients:
- 2 cups unsweetened almond milk
- ½ cup Goji berries
- ½ cup whole almonds, soaked
- 6 teaspoons of raw cacao powder
- 1 tablespoon of raw organic honey
- 3-4 ice cubes

Directions:
1. To you blender, add all the above ingredient and pulse until smooth.

Nutrition Info: (Per Serving): Calories- 440, Fat- 23 g, Protein- 16 g, Carbohydrates- 43 g

Berry Dessert Smoothie

Servings: 2
Cooking Time: 5 Minutes
Ingredients:
- ¼ cup unsweetened almond milk
- 1 cup low fat plain yogurt
- 1 cup strawberries (fresh or frozen)
- 1 cup blueberries (fresh or frozen)
- 1 large banana, chopped(fresh or frozen)
- 1 teaspoon freshly squeezed lemon juice
- ¼ teaspoon cinnamon powder
- 3-4 ice cubes

Directions:
1. Place all the above ingredients into the blender jar and process until the mixture is thick and creamy.

Nutrition Info: (Per Serving): Calories- 265, Fat- 3.8 g, Protein- 10 g, Carbohydrates- 50 g

Pink Grapefruit Skin

Servings: 3
Cooking Time: 5 Minutes
Ingredients:
- 1 cups pineapple, chopped
- 1 small grapefruit, peeled and chopped
- 1 cups cucumber, chopped
- A handful of cilantro, washed and chopped
- ¾ cups freshly squeezed orange juice
- Freshly squeezed juice of ½ lime
- ½ teaspoon vanilla extract
- A pinch of cinnamon powder

- A pinch of sea salt
- ½ teaspoon raw organic honey
- 3-4 ice cubes

Directions:
1. Place all the above ingredients into the blender jar and process until the mixture is thick and creamy.

Nutrition Info: (Per Serving): Calories- 44, Fat- 0.5 g, Protein- 1 g, Carbohydrates- 9.1g

Bluberry Cucumber Cooler

Servings: 2
Cooking Time: 5 Minutes
Ingredients:
- 1 cup whole blueberries (fresh or frozen)
- 1 cup unsweetened almond milk
- ½ cup cucumber, chopped
- 2 large lettuce leaves
- 2 teaspoons hemp seeds
- 1 teaspoon raw organic honey (optional)
- 3-4 ice cubes

Directions:
1. Place all the ingredients into your blender and whirr it on high for 20 seconds or until the desired consistency has been reached. Pour into glasses and serve immediately.

Nutrition Info: (Per Serving): Calories- 202, Fat- 7.2 g, Protein- 6 g, Carbohydrates- 30 g

Saffron Oats Smoothie

Servings: 2-3
Cooking Time: 5 Minutes
Ingredients:
- 2 ripe banana, sliced (fresh or frozen)
- 1 cup fresh coconut water
- 1 teaspoon raw organic honey
- 2 tablespoons oats
- ½ teaspoon vanilla extract
- A pinch of saffron
- ½ teaspoon of almond or cashew flakes (optional)

Directions:
1. Place everything in the blender jar, secure the lid and pulse until smooth.

Nutrition Info: (Per Serving): Calories- 136, Fat- 1.2 g, Protein- 1.3 g, Carbohydrates- 33 g

Pumpkin Spice Smoothie

Servings: 2
Cooking Time: 5 Minutes
Ingredients:

- 1 cup pumpkin, chopped
- ¾ cup plain yogurt
- 2 tablespoons avocado flesh
- 2 tablespoons flax seed powder
- ¼ pinch nutmeg powder
- A pinch of cinnamon powder
- A pinch of cayenne pepper
- ½ cup filtered water

Directions:
1. Pour all the items into the blender, secure the lid and blitz until the smoothie has reached a desired consistency and there are no lumps in the mixture. Pour into serving glasses and serve.
Nutrition Info: (Per Serving): Calories- 350, Fat- 15 g, Protein- 26 g, Carbohydrates- 39 g

Aloe Berry Smoothie

Servings: 2
Cooking Time: 2 Minutes
Ingredients:
- ½ cup blueberries (fresh or frozen)
- 1/3 cup fresh and pure aloe gel or aloe Vera juice
- 2 tablespoons avocado flesh
- A handful of dandelion greens, chopped
- 1 kiwi, peeled and chopped
- 1 teaspoon coconut oil
- 1 teaspoon cacao powder
- A pinch of Celtic salt
- 1 ½ teaspoons of raw organic honey
- 1 cup filtered water

Directions:
1. Combine all the ingredients in a blender, secure the lid firmly and blitz until smooth.
Nutrition Info: (Per Serving): Calories- 305, Fat- 15 g, Protein- 2.1 g, Carbohydrates- 45 g

Kale And Pomegranate Smoothie

Servings: 3
Cooking Time: 5 Minutes
Ingredients:
- 2/3 cup freshly prepared pomegranate juice
- 1/3 cup unsweetened almond milk
- 1 cup fresh kale, stems removed and chopped
- ¼ cup blueberries (fresh or frozen)
- ¼ cup raspberries (fresh or frozen)
- 1 ripe banana, chopped
- A handful of mixed greens
- 1 tablespoon of hemp seeds
- 1 teaspoon agave nectar

- 1 cup filtered water
- 3-4 ice cubes

Directions:

1. Place all the above ingredients into the blender jar and process until the mixture is thick and creamy.

Nutrition Info: (Per Serving): Calories- 185, Fat- 0.5 g, Protein- 3.5 g, Carbohydrates- 40 g

Cantaloupe Yogurt Smoothie

Servings: 1 Large
Cooking Time: 2 Minutes
Ingredients:

- 1 cup cantaloupe, chopped
- 1/3 cup plain yogurt
- ¼ teaspoon freshly grated ginger
- A pinch of nutmeg powder
- 1 tablespoon raw organic honey
- 1 teaspoon freshly squeezed lemon juice
- 3-4 mint leaves
- ½ cup filtered water
- 6-7 ice cubes

Directions:

1. Place everything into a blender and blitz until smooth. Pour into a glass and enjoy!

Nutrition Info: (Per Serving): Calories- 90, Fat- 0.9 g, Protein- 3.1 g, Carbohydrates- 20 g

Grape And Strawberry Smoothie

Servings: 2
Cooking Time: 5 Minutes
Ingredients:

- ½ cup whole strawberries (fresh or frozen)
- ½ cup red grapes, seedless
- 1 cup baby spinach, washed
- 1 cup mixed greens
- 2 tablespoons avocado flesh
- 2 teaspoons almond butter
- 1 teaspoon flax seed powder
- ¼ cup freshly squeezed lemon juice
- ¾ cup filtered water
- 2-3 ice cubes

Directions:

1. Whizz all the ingredients in the blender until smooth and serve.

Nutrition Info: (Per Serving): Calories- 310, Fat- 2 g, Protein- 8 g, Carbohydrates- 26 g

Pink Potion

Servings: 3-4
Cooking Time: 5 Minutes
Ingredients:
- 2 cups raw beet, peeled and chopped
- 2 cups whole strawberries (fresh or frozen)
- 2 tablespoons almond butter
- 2 fresh kale leaves stems removed and chopped
- 1 banana, sliced (fresh or frozen)
- 1 teaspoon vanilla extract
- 1 tablespoon hemp seeds
- 1 cup filtered water

Directions:
1. Place all the ingredients into the blender and whiz up until the smoothie is nice and thick.

Nutrition Info: (Per Serving): Calories- 285, Fat- 11 g, Protein- 9.9 g, Carbohydrates- 40 g

Nutty Raspberry Avocado Blend

Servings: 2
Cooking Time: 5 Minutes
Ingredients:
- 1 cup whole raspberries (fresh or frozen)
- 3/4 cup avocado, peeled, pitted and chopped
- 3/4 cup cashews, soaked
- 1 tablespoon organic coconut oil
- 1 ½ - 2 cups filtered water
- A pinch of Himalayan salt

Directions:
1. Dump all the ingredients into the blender and whip it up until the smoothie is thick and creamy.

Nutrition Info: (Per Serving): Calories- 698, Fat- 54 g, Protein- 9.1 g, Carbohydrates- 53 g

ENERGY BOOSTING SMOOTHIES

Ginger- Pomegranate Smoothie

Servings: 2
Cooking Time: 2 Minutes
Ingredients:
- 1 cup freshly prepared homemade pomegranate juice
- 4 ounces of plain Greek yogurt
- 1 large banana, chopped (fresh or frozen)
- ¼ teaspoon freshly grated ginger
- 1 teaspoon freshly squeezed lemon juice
- 3-4 ice cubes

Directions:
1. Pour all the ingredients into the blender and puree until smooth and frothy.

Nutrition Info: (Per Serving): Calories- 192, Fat- 2.1 g, Protein- 7.8 g, Carbohydrates- 40 g

Coco- Cranberry Smoothie

Servings: 3
Cooking Time: 5 Minutes
Ingredients:
- 1 cup fresh coconut water
- ½ green avocado, peeled and chopped
- ¼ cup mango, chopped
- ½ cup fresh spinach, chopped
- ½ cup kale, stems removed and chopped
- ¼ cup papaya, chopped
- 1/3cup plain yogurt
- ¼ cup cranberries(fresh , frozen or dried)
- ¼ cup Goji berries
- 1 teaspoon wheatgrass powder
- 1 tablespoon maca root powder
- 1 teaspoon pure coconut oil
- 1 teaspoon raw, organic honey

Directions:
1. Add all the ingredients one by one into your blender jar, secure the lid and run it on high for 30 seconds or until done.

Nutrition Info: (Per Serving): Calories- 531, Fat- 32 g, Protein- 15 g, Carbohydrates- 65 g

Persimmon Pineapple Protein Smoothie

Servings: 2
Cooking Time: 5 Minutes
Ingredients:
- 1 persimmon, topped and chopped
- 1 tablespoon cinnamon
- 1 squash

- 1 tablespoon flaxseed
- 4 ounces pineapple
- 1 tablespoon pea protein
- 1 cup of water

Directions:
1. Add all the listed ingredients to a blender
2. Blend until you have a smooth and creamy texture
3. Serve chilled and enjoy!

Nutrition Info: Calories: 159; Fat: 2g; Carbohydrates: 33g; Protein: 7g

Berry- Mint Cooler

Servings: 2
Cooking Time: 2 Minutes
Ingredients:
- 2 cups unsweetened almond milk
- A large handful of frozen blueberries
- 1 ½ teaspoons of raw, organic honey
- 1 ½ teaspoon flax seed powder
- 3-4 fresh mint leaves
- 4-5 ice cubes

Directions:
1. To your high speed blender, add all the ingredients and process for 30 seconds or until done.

Nutrition Info: (Per Serving): Calories- 201, Fat-7.2 g, Protein-11 g, Carbohydrates- 21 g

Powerful Green Frenzy

Servings: 2
Cooking Time: 5 Minutes
Ingredients:
- 1 cup ice
- 2 tablespoons almond butter
- 1 teaspoon spirulina
- 3 teaspoons fresh ginger
- 1½ frozen bananas, sliced
- 2 cups baby spinach, chopped
- 1 cup kale
- 1½ cups unsweetened almond milk

Directions:
1. Add all the ingredients except vegetables/fruits first
2. Blend until smooth
3. Add the vegetable/fruits
4. Blend until smooth
5. Add a few ice cubes and serve the smoothie
6. Enjoy!

Nutrition Info: Calories: 350; Fat: 4g; Carbohydrates: 54g; Protein: 30g

Mango Beet Energy Booster

Servings: 2
Cooking Time: 5 Minutes
Ingredients:
- ½ cup unsweetened almond milk
- 1 cup red beet, peeled and chopped
- 1 ripe banana, chopped (fresh or frozen)
- 1 small mango, peeled and chopped
- 2 cups baby spinach, chopped
- ½ teaspoon freshly grated giber
- A handful of ice cubes

Directions:
1. Load your blender with all the ingredients mentioned above and run it on medium high for 45 seconds until there are no lumps. Pour into beautiful glasses and serve.

Nutrition Info: (Per Serving): Calories- 165, Fat- 1.1 g, Protein- 4 g, Carbohydrates- 40 g

Generous Mango Surprise

Servings: 2
Cooking Time: 5 Minutes
Ingredients:
- 1 tablespoon spirulina
- 3 cups frozen mango, sliced
- 1½ cups kale
- 2½ cups unsweetened almond milk

Directions:
1. Add all the ingredients except vegetables/fruits first
2. Blend until smooth
3. Add the vegetable/fruits
4. Blend until smooth
5. Add a few ice cubes and serve the smoothie
6. Enjoy!

Nutrition Info: Calories: 72; Fat: 0g; Carbohydrates: 17g; Protein: 1g

Almond-banana Booster

Servings: 2
Cooking Time: 5 Minutes
Ingredients:
- 2 large banana, chopped (fresh or frozen)
- 1 cup unsweetened almond milk
- A handful of almonds
- ¼ cup plain Greek yogurt
- 2 tablespoons Chia seeds, soaked
- 1 teaspoon hemp seed powder
- 2 teaspoons freshly squeezed lemon juice

- 1 teaspoon raw organic honey
- A handful of ice cubes

Directions:

1. Pour everything into the blender and process for 30 seconds until nice and thick.

Nutrition Info: (Per Serving): Calories- 244, Fat- 6.2 g, Protein- 7 g, Carbohydrates- 32 g

Banana Apple Blast

Servings: 2
Cooking Time: 5 Minutes
Ingredients:

- 1 cup ice
- 1 teaspoon bee pollen
- 1 teaspoon spirulina
- 1 cup fresh pineapple, sliced
- 1 frozen banana, sliced
- 2 cups baby spinach
- 1½ cups unsweetened coconut milk drink

Directions:

1. Add all the ingredients except vegetables/fruits first
2. Blend until smooth
3. Add the vegetable/fruits
4. Blend until smooth
5. Add a few ice cubes and serve the smoothie
6. Enjoy!

Nutrition Info: Calories: 209; Fat: 2g; Carbohydrates: 51g; Protein: 2g

Mct Strawberry Smoothie

Servings: 2
Cooking Time: 10 Minutes
Ingredients:

- 1 and ¼ cups of coconut milk
- 4 tablespoons strawberry
- ½ cup heavy whipping cream
- 14 large ice cubes
- ½ teaspoon xanthan gum
- 2 tablespoons MCT oil

Directions:

1. Add all the listed ingredients to a blender
2. Blend until you have a smooth and creamy texture
3. Serve chilled and enjoy!

Nutrition Info: Calories: 373; Fat: 45.1g; Carbohydrates: 5.8g; Protein: 2.1g

Mango Honey Smoothie

Servings: 2

Cooking Time: 10 Minutes
Ingredients:
- 2 mangoes, peeled, pit removed and chopped
- 4 teaspoons honey
- 3 cups almond milk
- 16 ice cubes

Directions:
1. Add all the listed ingredients to a blender
2. Blend until you have a smooth and creamy texture
3. Serve chilled and enjoy!

Nutrition Info: Calories: 223; Fat: 3.4g; Carbohydrates: 49.2g; Protein: 2.9g

Berry Flax Smoothie

Servings: 4
Cooking Time: 10 Minutes
Ingredients:
- 3 cups dairy-free milk
- 2 cups spinach
- 2 tablespoons flaxseeds, ground
- 1 cup berries, fresh or frozen
- 2 teaspoons ginger root, peeled

Directions:
1. Add all the listed ingredients to a blender
2. Blend until you have a smooth and creamy texture
3. Serve chilled and enjoy!

Nutrition Info: Calories: 212; Fat: 11.9g; Carbohydrates: 31.7g; Protein: 7.3g

DIABETES SMOOTHIES

Cucumber-kale Chiller

Servings: 2
Cooking Time: 5 Minutes
Ingredients:
- 1 cup fresh coconut milk
- ½ cup cucumber, chopped
- ½ cup pineapple, chopped
- 2 kiwi frits, peeled and chopped
- 2/3 cup fresh kale, stems removed and chopped
- 2 tablespoon freshly squeezed lime juice
- 1 teaspoon freshly squeezed lemon juice
- 3-4 ice cubes

Directions:
1. Place all the above listed items in the blender jar, secure the lid and whizz until smooth.

Nutrition Info: (Per Serving): Calories- 106, Fat- 6.5 g, Protein-5 g, Carbohydrates- 53 g

Berry Truffle Smoothie

Servings: 2
Cooking Time: 10 Minutes
Ingredients:
- 1 medium Haas avocado
- 1 and ¼ teaspoons pure vanilla extract
- ½ cup whipping cream
- 3 tablespoons cocoa powder, unsweetened
- 4 tablespoons pecans
- 1 and ¼ cups mixed berries, frozen
- 2 pinches salt
- ¾ cups of ice cubes
- Erythritol, to taste
- 1 cup of water

Directions:
1. Add all the listed ingredients to a blender
2. Blend until you have a smooth and creamy texture
3. Serve chilled and enjoy!

Nutrition Info: Calories: 375; Fat: 32.5g; Carbohydrates: 11.3g; Protein: 5.8g

Berry-licious Meta Booster

Servings: 2
Cooking Time: 5 Minutes
Ingredients:
- ¼ cup garbanzo bean
- 1 teaspoon flax oil
- ½ cup frozen blueberries

- ½ cup frozen broccoli florets
- 6 ounces Greek yogurt
- ¾ cup brewed and chilled green tea

Directions:
1. Add all the ingredients except vegetables/fruits first
2. Blend until smooth
3. Add the vegetable/fruits
4. Blend until smooth
5. Add a few ice cubes and serve the smoothie
6. Enjoy!

Nutrition Info: Calories: 200; Fat: 3g; Carbohydrates: 41g; Protein: 5g

Plum- Bokchoy Smoothie

Servings: 2
Cooking Time: 5 Minutes
Ingredients:
- 1 cup kale, stems removed and chopped
- 1 banana, chopped (fresh or frozen)
- 1 medium head bok choy
- 1 large red plum, pitted and chopped
- 2 tablespoons avocado flesh
- 2 teaspoons freshly squeezed lime juice
- ½ cup filtered water
- 2-3 ice cubes

Directions:
1. Load the high speed bender with all the ingredients and pulse until smooth.

Nutrition Info: (Per Serving): Calories- 260, Fat-10 g, Protein- 8 g, Carbohydrates- 45 g

Keto Mocha Smoothie

Servings: 4
Cooking Time: 10 Minutes
Ingredients:
- 6 tablespoons cocoa powder, unsweetened
- 1 cup of coconut milk
- 3 cups almond milk, unsweetened
- 2 avocados, cut in half
- 2 teaspoons vanilla extract
- 6 tablespoons erythritol, granulated
- 4 teaspoons instant coffee crystals

Directions:
1. Add all the listed ingredients to a blender
2. Blend until you have a smooth and creamy texture
3. Serve chilled and enjoy!

Nutrition Info: Calories: 273; Fat: 24.3g; Carbohydrates: 8.2g; Protein: 4.5g

Avocado Turmeric Smoothie

Servings: 1
Cooking Time: 10 Minutes
Ingredients:
- 1 avocado
- 2 teaspoons lemon juice
- 1 teaspoon turmeric
- 2 teaspoons ginger, fresh grated
- 1 and ¼ cups of coconut milk
- 2 cups ice, crushed
- Stevia, to taste

Directions:
1. Add all the listed ingredients to a blender
2. Blend until you have a smooth and creamy texture
3. Serve chilled and enjoy!

Nutrition Info: Calories: 320; Fat: 27.4g; Carbohydrates: 11g; Protein: 4.3g

Oat, Celery Green Smoothie

Servings: 2
Cooking Time: 5 Minutes
Ingredients:
- ¾ cup unsweetened almond milk
- ¼ cup tightly packed spinach, washed and chopped
- ¼ cup cucumber, chopped
- ½ cup whole strawberries (fresh or frozen)
- ¼ cup whole strawberries (fresh or frozen)
- 1 celery stalk, chopped
- 4 teaspoons rolled oats
- 1 ½ teaspoon cacao powder
- 1 ½ teaspoon flax seed powder
- ½ teaspoon cinnamon powder
- 4-5 ice cubes

Directions:
1. Load your blender jar with the above listed items and process until smooth.

Nutrition Info: (Per Serving): Calories- 340, Fat- 12.3 g, Protein- 13.1 g, Carbohydrates- 47 g

Hemp And Kale Smoothie

Servings: 2
Cooking Time: 5 Minutes
Ingredients:
- 1 large banana, chopped (fresh or frozen)
- A large handful of baby spinach, washed and chopped
- A large handful of kale, stems removed and chopped
- 1 tablespoon of hemp seeds

- 2-3 drops of liquid Stevia (optional)
- 2 teaspoons of freshly squeezed lemon juice
- 1 ½ cups of filtered water

Directions:

1. Place all the ingredients in the blender jar, secure the lid and pulse it for 20 seconds until everything is well combined.

Nutrition Info: (Per Serving): Calories- 340, Fat- 16 g, Protein- 15 g, Carbohydrates- 44 g

Strawberry – Banana Smoothie

Servings: 2
Cooking Time: 5 Minutes

Ingredients:

- 2 small heads of bok choy
- 2 cups whole strawberries (fresh or frozen)
- 1 large banana, chopped (fresh or frozen)
- 2 tablespoon avocado flesh
- 1 teaspoon flax seed powder
- ½ cup filtered water

Directions:

1. Combine all the ingredients in the blender and pulse until smooth

Nutrition Info: (Per Serving): Calories- 290, Fat- 10 g, Protein- 6.2 g, Carbohydrates- 55 g

Parsley- Pineapple Smoothie

Servings: 2
Cooking Time: 5 Minutes

Ingredients:

- ¾ cup fresh kale, stems removed and chopped
- 1 cup pineapple, chopped
- 1 small banana, chopped (fresh or frozen)
- ½ cup whole strawberries (fresh or frozen)
- A handful of parsley , washed
- 1 teaspoon of hemp seed powder
- 1 teaspoon freshly squeezed lemon juice
- 5-6 ice cubes

Directions:

1. Place all the above mentioned items into the blender jar and run it on medium high for 30 seconds or until smoothie is thick and frothy.

Nutrition Info: (Per Serving): Calories- 440, Fat-8.1 g, Protein- 15 g, Carbohydrates- 94.5 g

Choco Spinach Delight

Servings: 1
Cooking Time: 10 Minutes

Ingredients:

- 4 ice cubes
- 1 scoop green superfood
- 1 scoop protein powder
- 1 tablespoon chia seeds
- ½ cup berry yogurt
- 1 handful of organic spinach
- 1 teaspoon organic flaxseed
- ½ avocado
- 1/3 cup organic strawberries, frozen
- ½ cup organic blueberries, frozen
- ¾ cup unsweetened almond milk

Directions:
1. Add all the listed ingredients to a blender
2. Blend until you have a smooth and creamy texture
3. Serve chilled and enjoy!

Nutrition Info: Calories: 180; Fat: 16g; Carbohydrates: 7g; Protein: 1g

CPSIA information can be obtained
at www.ICGtesting.com
Printed in the USA
BVHW071408091221
623632BV00005B/90